Built by the Lord

Edwin Crozier

Built by the Lord: A Study of the Family

P.O. Box 6259, Chillicothe, Ohio 45601
800.300.9778
www.deward.com

First published by Streamside Supplies in 2005.

Cover design by Jonathan Hardin.

Printed in the United States of America.

ISBN: 978-1-936341-21-2

Contents

Introduction

How important is your family? What are you willing to do to make your family stable and functional? Are you willing to work long hours to provide materially for your family? Are you willing to rise up early and stay up late to accomplish all the goals and activities in which your family is involved? Are you willing to eat the bread of painful labors to give your children a better life? Are you willing to pursue education, material goods, comfort and recreation for your family? Will you read books? …watch videos? …visit counselors? How important is a stable and functional family to you?

Here is the important question: Is having a stable and functional family important enough to allow the Lord to build your home?

> *Unless the Lord builds the house,*
> *They labor in vain who build it;*
> *Unless the Lord guards the city,*
> *The watchman keeps awake in vain.*
> *It is vain for you to rise up early,*
> *To retire late,*
> *To eat the bread of painful labors;*
> *For he gives to His beloved even in his sleep*
> *Psalm 127.1–2*

All of the things we are willing to do to stabilize and functionalize our families are no more than wheel-spinning unless we are willing to allow God to come into our homes, building them and guarding them His way. Are we willing to allow that?

This book is a five week focus on the family. We want our homes to be built by the Lord and I pray that this book will be a tool to help you accomplish that goal. Do you remember the "children's" song we sing based on Matthew 7.24–27? The wise man built his house upon the rock. The floods came and the winds blew and the wise man's house stood firm. Let's face it, storms and earthquakes are coming. There is nothing we are going to do to stop them. However, when the Lord builds our house and we build it on the foundation of the Lord, our families will weather those storms and earthquakes.

I encourage you to read through this book one chapter every weekday for the next five weeks. It has been divided into five week long sections—*First Things, Family Goals, Family Roles, Habits of a God-built Home, Our Family and God's Family.* At the end of each reading you will find a Response, a Point to Ponder and a Prayer. Work through those exercises each day to help implement the Bible's lessons in your life.

While I believe you will receive a great deal of benefit by working through this book on your own or with your own family, I highly encourage you to develop an accountability circle. This book is designed not only as a family devotional and lesson book, but also as a small group study guide. Develop a circle of friends and family who will read through this book and get together to discuss what you have learned, what questions you have and what help you can give each other. At the end of each week-long section, I have included a small group discussion guide.

The most beneficial aspect of the group discussion is the questions are not designed to say, "Here are the seven most important lessons the author wanted you to get." Instead, these questions are designed to promote discussion regarding what you found to be most important and to allow you, your family and your brethren to seek and offer help regarding what you found most difficult.

If you decide not to be involved with an accountability group or are not able to be, please do not skip those discussion questions. Work through them by yourself or with your family. They will help you summarize what you have learned and delineate the areas on which you want and need to work the hardest.

I hope I can convey the proper tone throughout this book. At times, I have written on very difficult topics and made some very difficult statements. I trust you realize my family is not perfect. I wish I could say, "Look at my family, we have always done all these things and see how awesome we are." That is simply not the case.

This has been a work of Bible study, not a work of personal family research. The chapters in this book represent what I believe the Bible teaches to be the family ideal, not what my family is.

Developing this material was a growth process. Going through it with my family and home congregation for the first time was a further growth process. Editing this book for publication was an even further growth process. Being reminded by my children about what we read in "that book you wrote" has been an even further growth process. To illustrate this, when you get to chapter 8, "Relationship Goal #1: Love," the Response will ask you to work through an exercise based on 1 Corinthians 13.4–7, replacing the word "love" with your name, e.g. Edwin is kind... You will be asked to take it a step further and include someone in your family as an object of the sentence, e.g. Edwin is kind to Marita (my wife). When we worked through that exercise and I included my name as the subject and my wife's as the object, I read through the entire passage. I certainly knew what I said did not accurately reflect the way I behave all the time. However, I was not prepared for my eight-year old daughter, Tessa, to immediately say, "There were a lot of lies in that, Dad." I have a lot of work to do and even my kids can see that.

I am confessing this to you to let you know where I stand. Please do not regard this book as the work of some professor who has figured out all the answers and is getting it right all the time. Like you, I am a pilgrim progressing through this world as best I can, relying on God and studying His word to help me grow. This book is not a family manual, but a tool pointing to the family manual—the Bible. I pray it will be a blessing to you and help your family be a blessing to God.

Before moving directly into the meat of this book, learning about the goals, roles and habits of a God-built family, I would like to share five lessons I have learned from Psalm 127 about allowing the Lord to build our homes.

Because of Psalm 127.3–5, we almost universally apply this psalm to the family (of course, we do this because the psalm does apply to the family). However, when we examine this psalm in its historical context, we gain insight from a different angle, providing a great illustration for us. This psalm is attributed to Solomon. With that in mind, we cannot help but think of the great house about which Solomon was most concerned to build—the Temple, the house of Jehovah God. Further, as king, we can't help but thing Solomon had a particular city in mind as he wrote this psalm—Jerusalem. To add to this picture, this psalm is in the "Songs of Ascent" section. This was one of the psalms the Jews sang as they traveled on their annual pilgrimages to Jerusalem for the feasts of the Lord. They sang this psalm as they prepared to worship at the house of God in the city of God. This psalm was first and foremost about the Temple of God, the City of God and the Nation of God. Yet this nation was itself a family. Just as God would deal with the nation, its capital and its house of worship, so does God deal with the individual family. With this historical context in mind, I believe we learn some fascinating lessons from the building and rebuilding of the Lord's House and City. Lessons we can apply them to our own families.

First, if we want the Lord to build our homes, we must invite Him to do so. He will not force our family to do anything. In 1 Chronicles 29.10–19, David prayed that God would strengthen Solomon to complete the work for which David had prepared. Further, in 2 Chronicles 6, Solomon prayed that God make all their work on the temple worthwhile by accepting it as a place of worship. Without inviting God into the temple, David's preparation and Solomon's work would have been meaningless. However, they invited God to be a part of it and God demonstrated that He accepted their invitation in 2 Chronicles 7.

Second, 1 Chronicles 28.19 says, "'All this,' said David, 'the Lord made me understand in writing by His hand upon me, all the details of the pattern.'" The design of God's temple was not left up to man, Solomon was to follow God's pattern. If we want the Lord to build and guard our homes, we must follow His pattern. This is not about what feels right to us. It is not about what we want or what society has determined. This is not about cultural norms and taboos, it is about God's word and pattern.

These first two lessons are the bedrock. If our families will be built by the Lord, they must be praying and Bible-applying families.

Third, we must not push Psalm 127.2 farther than God intended it to go. This psalm teaches that without God's involvement our work is vain. Further, it teaches that God blesses His servants even when they are resting. However, this psalm does not intend to teach that if we simply pray and read our Bibles, God will do everything else and we do not need to work. In fact, when we see Nehemiah rebuilding the city of God and relying on God to guard the city, we read two powerful verses. Nehemiah 2.18 says, "Then they said, 'Let us arise and build.' So they put their hands to the good work." Then Nehemiah 4.6 says, "So we built the wall and the whole was joined together to half its height, for the people had a mind to work." If the Lord will build our homes, we must have a mind to work and we must put our hands to the work.

Fourth, when the Jews returned to Jerusalem from the captivity, they almost immediately began to rebuild the House of the Lord. Their enemies discouraged them. Building stopped. I am sure at first they were sorrowful and looked for opportunity to restart the building. However, based on Haggai 1.1–8, it appears they became complacent. They became complacent, being distracted by all the mundane and material things of their life. Therefore they procrastinated the more important spiritual work. How easy it is to get distracted with the mundane and material issues of everyday life under the sun. We must not allow these things to distract us from God's things. As Colossians 3.2 says, we must set our mind on the things above and not on the things on earth.

Fifth, as important as the house and city of God were, we have to ask why did God abandon them—not once, but twice? If the Lord built the house and the Lord guarded the city, nothing should have happened to them. Why then is the temple in ruins and the city a warzone? Despite all the good examples set by God's people providing the basis for our first four points, God's people stopped serving Him. Read Daniel's confession in Daniel 9.4–19. The Lord abandoned His house and His city, because the people abandoned Him. If we want the Lord to build and guard our home, we must always serve the Lord. We must not bank on past service and submission. We have not obligated God to us through our past work. If we abandon God, He will eventually abandon us.

Psalm 127 is the basis and inspiration of this entire book. We want our homes to be Built by the Lord. Please allow these lessons from that chapter to be the compass for all you do in your family.

Again, I pray this book will be a blessing to you and will help you and your family be a blessing to God. I am excited to learn these lessons with you. Let's get to it by starting on week one: *First Things*.

Week One:
First Things

"God created man in His own image, in the image of God He created him; male and female He created them. God blessed them; and God said to them, 'Be fruitful and multiply, and fill the earth, and subdue it; and rule over the fish of the sea and over the birds of the sky and over every living thing that moves on the earth."

Genesis 1.27–28

Week 1

1

God Created the Home

In the Beginning...

"In the beginning God created the heavens and the earth." I hardly need place the reference beside this quote. Who does not know Genesis 1.1?

The earth was formless and void but God added light, divided waters, caused dry land to appear and created life. On the sixth day, God created "living creatures after their kind; cattle and creeping things and beasts of the earth after their kind" (Genesis 1.24).

God then made another creature, "Let Us make man in Our image, according to Our likeness..." (Genesis 1.26–27). Genesis 2.7, 18–24 reviews this creation and describes man's creation from the dust of the ground more fully. However, despite all the creatures God had made, none were suitable as man's companion. Therefore, God created woman.

So the Lord God caused a deep sleep to fall upon the man, and he slept; then He took one of his ribs and closed up the flesh at that place. The Lord God fashioned into a woman the rib which He had taken from the man, and brought her to the man. The man said, 'This is now bone of my bones, and flesh of my flesh; she shall be called Woman, because she was taken out of Man.' For this reason a man shall leave his father and his mother, and be joined to his wife; and they shall become one flesh" (Genesis 2.21–24).

When God created woman, He also created the family. As Moses commented on this creation, he mentioned not only husbands and wives, but mothers and fathers and, by implication, children. Thus, the family is the very first institution God brought into the world.

Do you see how important this concept is? The family is not a product of evolution. Nor was the family a cultural creation by some ancient society to provide and govern legal benefits.

The family is as old as mankind, because God created it alongside mankind.

Since man did not create the family, man does not define or govern how the family is supposed to work. With the modern debate over homosexuality, many are looking to how families have been organized throughout the numerous historical cultures. It does not matter how various cultures organized their families. What matters is how God organized the family. Anything else, no matter how widespread, is a perversion of how the family should exist.

The point is very simple. God created the family. Therefore, God governs the family. He not only governs the family in a general sense, He governs your family and my family particularly. Paul drove this home in 1 Corinthians 11.3, "But I want you to understand that Christ is the head of every man, and the man is the head of a woman, and God is the head of Christ." While we know the head of the family in one sense is the husband and father, we must recognize the ultimate head and shepherd of every family is God.

This flies in the face of what most people want—at least in American culture. Most believe what goes on in their family is their business and no one else's. The reality is what goes on in every family is God's business. He has the right to tell us what to do in our families.

That is what this study is about. What has God told us to do in our families? Every question we answer about the family needs to come back to this anchor? The anchor is not what we think or feel about the family. It is not what we are sure God must think about it or what the societal mood about it is. The anchor is what God said about it.

The Church and the Family

In this regard, the family is very much like the church. God instituted the church on Pentecost following Christ's resurrection (Acts 2). He established roles and offices within that body. Ephesians 4.11 says, "He gave some as apostles, and some as prophets, and some as evangelists, and some as pastors and teachers."

He established local congregations, readily seen throughout the New Testament. He established leadership in those congregations. Paul's missionary work demonstrated this in Acts 14.23, "When they had appointed elders for them in every church..." Peter described these elders as shepherds in 1 Peter 5.1–2 saying, "Therefore, I exhort the elders among you…shepherd the flock of God among you…"

However, these shepherds were, and are, not a rule unto themselves. They are not to govern the congregation in whatever way they see fit. They have no authority to develop doctrine or devise policy. As Peter states in 1 Peter 5.4, there is a Chief Shepherd. That Chief Shepherd is Jesus.

According to Matthew 28.18, "Jesus came up and spoke to them, saying, 'All authority has been given to Me in heaven and on earth.'" Paul drove the point home further in Ephesians 1.22–23, writing, "And He [the Father] put all things in subjection under His [the Son's] feet, and gave Him as head over all things to the church..."

God supplied offices of leadership within the church, but these are subject to the real leader, Jesus Christ. Who is, of course, subject to the Father—"But when He says, 'All things are put in subjection,' it is evident that He is excepted who put all things in subjection to Him" (1 Corinthians 15.27).

The church does not get to do whatever it wants, but what its Head wants. Most would acknowledge this point. The same is true for the family. Just as God is the head of His church and gets to rule over it. God, as Creator, is head of the family and gets to rule over it. The question is will we let Him rule or follow our own lead?

The Family Goal

In week two of our study, we are going to dig more deeply into what the goals of every family ought to be. However, for now, we realize the overarching goal of each family is pleasing God.

Jesus provided the proper example for us in John 8.29, "He who sent Me is with Me; He has not left Me alone, for I always do the things that are pleasing to Him."

We hear a lot about functional and dysfunctional families in the modern media. No matter how it appears on the outside, a family is only functional when it pleases God. The family members may get along fine. The parents may make lots of money. The kids may be doing well in school. Yet, if God is not being pleased in their home, they are as dysfunctional as the proverbial alcoholic home.

The tough part about this is pleasing God does not come naturally.

It takes effort and purpose. It is a lot like your house. What would happen if you quit cleaning your house, cutting the grass and fixing whatever breaks? The house would become more and more run down. That is exactly the way our families work. If we do not perform the upkeep, the family will run down.

Spirituality in the home does not happen all on its own. In fact, it has a tendency to dissipate. That is, if you don't work on it, it will disappear. Further, it often seems if the parents become only half-hearted Christians, their children will almost certainly become apathetic toward spiritual matters.

That is why a study like this one is important. It will help us maintain a spiritual focus in our families. It will help us purposefully pay attention to whether or not God is being glorified in our homes. We have to be committed to this study, however, for it to work. We must commit right now to do our part of the daily study every weekday. We need to set a time for our families to read and discuss each day.

Unless the Lord Builds the House

The title for this book was inspired by Psalm 127.1: "Unless the Lord builds the house, they labor in vain who build it." This psalm demonstrates the true importance of having your home built upon the foundation of the Lord's will, pleasing Him.

If we are basing our home life on anything other than God's will and word, all we do is vain. It makes me think of the kids song we sing based on Matthew 7.24–27. The wise family builds its house upon the rock of Jesus' word. No doubt, we may live in nice houses. We may rub elbows with all the important people. But one day we will die and be face to face with the most important person in existence—not only us, but our spouses and our children. Is the focus of our family going to help us at all in that moment?

Further, this passage points out that God blesses His beloved even in their sleep (Psalm 127.3). When we build our home on God's principles, pleasing and glorifying Him, He works for us, securing our family and blessing us in ways we never imagined.

Certainly, we must recognize the words of this psalm are not intended to say if anyone has anything bad happen to them, their family life must be ungodly. This psalm is very much like the Proverbs. It provides a general truth, not an absolute statement. Just read Job to find that out.

In general, however, we learn God's guidelines for the home are for our benefit. When we do things His way, we will most often be blessed. Of course, when we do things His way, we will certainly be blessed eternally. In other words, this study is not simply another card to punch. Don't view this as dreaded "homework." Recognize that learning and being reminded of God's ways for the home is what will produce the greatest blessing for our families—now and eternally.

Commit to this study and improve your God-glorifying family, you won't regret it.

Today's Response:

Make your commitment:

We, the undersigned, commit to study this material in order to help our family please God.

____
Dad

____
Mom

____

____

____

____
Children

In the space below, schedule the time you and your family plan to read the material every weekday.

____

With whom will you be working to strengthen your family and hold you accountable in this period of study and focus on the family?

____

Point to Ponder:

Take a look at Psalm 127.2. Explain what you think that verse means and how it applies to your family in the space below.

Today's Prayer:

Father in heaven,

Thank You for the family and all the blessings provided through it. Thank You for our family and all the blessings we have received through it.

Please, build our home. Help us be pleasing to You. Father we love You and want to honor You in our home. Forgive us where we have fallen short in this and help us overcome the tempter.

We praise You for Your great grace in our family. We love you.

Through Your Son we pray,

Amen

Week 1

2

God's Institution for Impacting the World

Abraham's Family

Knowing our sinfulness and the ultimate destiny awaiting sinners, God developed a plan to bless the entire world. Interestingly, He began His world-impacting plan by picking one family.

Beginning with Abraham, God worked to build a family through whom He accomplished everything. Abraham and Sarah gave birth to Isaac. Isaac and Rebekah gave birth to Jacob, who became Israel. Israel and his wives and concubines gave birth to the heads of the twelve tribes of Israel.

God protected and built up this family in most amazing ways. He provided preservation from famine through Joseph, who had been sold into slavery, cast into prison and then lifted to power as second in Egypt. In the midst of slavery, He grew this family of 70 (Exodus 1.5) into a nation of 603,550 men, 20 years old and upward (Numbers 1.46). Through a series of miracles, God brought Israel out of Egypt. Finally, despite the rebellion from within and attacks from without, God brought this special nation into His Promised Land.

The story did not end there but as God continued to work with this one family, disciplining it, reining it in, blessing it and preserving it. Then He brought His Son into the world through this family to bless all the families of the world, including ours (Genesis 12.3).

When we take this bird's eye view of God's plan, we learn something immensely important about family. The family is the primary institution God has established to work His plans.

Certainly the church is a great teaching institution. Certainly God expects His church to impact the world, being the pillar and support of the truth (1 Timothy 3.15). However, the family is the primary unit through which God expects even the church to grow and accomplish its work.

Before our families can please God, we must understand the impact God expects them to have. We are not living in a vacuum. God expects our families to be God-glorifying, God-honoring units that spread the borders of His kingdom.

Bible Families

Think of how many times God worked through families. In Genesis 1–2, God did not create a civilization to populate the earth. He created a family.

In Genesis 6, when the thoughts of mankind had become only evil continually, God chose Noah, who had found grace in His eyes, and his family to preserve humanity in the ark.

In Leviticus 8, when God chose a priesthood to minister to Him and administer His law, He did not choose an individual but the family of Aaron.

When Joshua stood before the people to turn their hearts to God, he did not do it alone. He said, "As for me and my house, we will serve the Lord" (Joshua 24.15).

On the other hand, when an Israelite sinned, God often held his family accountable, punishing them as a unit. When Korah, Dathan and Abiram rebelled against Moses, God opened the earth around their entire families (Numbers 16.27–33). When Achan kept back part of the spoil of Jericho and hid it under his tent, the Israelites stoned his entire family (Joshua 7.24–25).

Can we doubt as we look through these narratives that God works through families? Do not misunderstand, certainly God works through individuals. If your family does not support your work in the Lord, He can still accomplish great things through you. The point is simply that God did not establish families so we could have wonderful relationships for a few years. He established families to be working units that impact the world for His glory.

Your family is no exception.

The Impact of Our Families

Have you ever thought of your family in this way? Far too often we think internally about families. That is, we think about all the things in the world that impact us. Even the most spiritual among us are often concerned about simply preserving their families from the impact of the world (an important goal-but we must not stop there).

With this mindset, we think about what we can use of the world to impact our families better. We focus on jobs and opportunities to provide income. If we have children, we think about education and entertainment to provide the best for them. We want to explore and experience all the opportunities we can for our betterment, entertainment and enjoyment.

Certainly, there is nothing wrong with some of that. On the whole, however, that is not the way God views our families. He views our families as teams that could grow into nations of servants like Abraham. Remember what God said about Abraham in Genesis 18.19, "For I have chosen him, so that he may command his children and his household after him to keep the way of the Lord by doing righteousness and justice..."

I recognize the very special place Abraham held in God's plan. I am not suggesting God has chosen to literally turn our families into another nation and bring about a promised blessing on the entire world through us. I am simply pointing out God has chosen us to have the same family mentality He expected from Abraham.

Our family is to be trained up in doing righteousness, to keep the way of the Lord. We are to train our children up to serve God. We are to train them up so they might train their children up and that they might train their children up and so on. Think of it this way. When we work on our own family in this way, even if all of our other efforts are fruitless, how many God-fearing, world impacting Christians will come from our family over the next several generations?

With simple math, we see what a generational legacy could produce. If you have only two children that you train up to serve the Lord and they each have two that they train up and so on. Assuming your descendants double in this fashion every 30 years, in 300 years there will be over 2000—a number that will continue to double every 30 years. In 600 years that number will be over 2 million descendents.

If we increase the number of children to three, in 300 years you will have over 177,000 and in 600 there will be over 10 billion.

I know; we probably cannot expect any family to keep producing faithfully like this for that many generations. Of course, we certainly cannot expect it if none of us try. God sees our families as units of kingdom growth and world impact. We need to see them that way.

Aside from the future demographic projections we also need to think about impact now. What do we expect from our families in God's service right now?

Galatians 6.10 says, "So then, while we have opportunity, let us do good to all people, and especially to those who are of the household of faith." Think about all the good your family could do for those around us.

Are there any elderly whose houses you could clean? Whose laundry you can wash? Whose lawns you could mow together? Are there any young couples for whom your teenage kids could babysit? Are there any sick for whom you could cook or clean? By the way, we are talking about good deeds here, not business ventures.

Imagine what impact your family could have if it was trained up as a miniature army for doing good. That is exactly what God intended.

Of course, we cannot leave this topic without talking about teaching. In 2 Timothy 2.2, Paul told Timothy, "The things which you have heard from me in the presence of many witnesses, entrust these to faithful men who will be able to teach others also."

If we ought to pass the teaching of Christ along to others so they can teach, how much more ought we to do this in our families? Think of the impact your immediate family can have in your larger family, in your community and in your congregation if one of your main goals is to pass along the gospel so your family can teach others also.

This is the kind of mindset God wants us to have for our families. Perhaps He will not make our family a great nation like Abraham's. But then again, who can fathom what the God who can do far more abundantly beyond all we ask or think (Ephesians 3.20) might do with a family that decides to impact the world for His glory?

Today's Response:

In the space below, make a list of some good deeds you and your family could do this week. Plan when you will do them.

Point to Ponder:

In Joshua 24.15, Joshua was able, with confidence, to claim that his house would serve the Lord with him. What kind of training do you think made that statement possible? What do you think you need to do in your family to be able to make a similar statement?

Today's Prayer:

Father in heaven,

We bless You because of Your awesome power and plan to save man. We are amazed that You accomplished Your plan through one family.

Father, we pray that our family will also be able to serve You as Abraham's did. Help us see the opportunities You have established for us to serve and glorify You.

Please forgive us if we have been self-centered in our family and help us look outwardly and learn to impact Your world, spreading the borders of Your kingdom.

We love you, Father.

Through Your Son we pray,

Amen

Seek First God's Kingdom and Righteousness

God's Kingdom and Righteousness

I have often thought about putting together a list of verses that have nothing to do with the family, but everything to do with the family. That is, the immediate context of the passage is not about family, but the principle should be upheld in the family more than any place else.

Matthew 6.33 would be at the top of that list. "But seek first His kingdom and His righteousness, and all these things will be added to you." The immediate context is about individual service. Yet, the principle applies to service within our families and to how the family ought to function as a whole.

Our families are to seek God's kingdom and righteousness. But what does that mean? Should we begin a worldwide trek hunting down the nation of God? Is this like all those stories or jokes we hear of people who hunt down the wise sage in the middle of the desert or on the top of the mountain?

Luke 17.21 reads, "Nor will they say, 'Look, here it is!' or, 'There it is!' For behold, the kingdom of God is in your midst." Or as the King James Version says, "...the kingdom of God is within you." As Jesus told Pilate, God's kingdom is not a physical kingdom with land, territories and borders (John 18.36). It is a spiritual kingdom. Its territory does not cover the face of the earth but the hearts of men.

Seeking God's kingdom means seeking God's rule in our hearts, or rather, seeking the King's dominion in our lives.

God's righteousness is demonstrated in Philippians 3.8–9. Paul wrote, "...so that I may gain Christ, and may be found in Him, not having a righteousness of my own derived from the

Law, but that which is through faith in Christ, the righteousness which comes from God on the basis of faith."

Faith is the conviction that God's way is the right way. Faith is the guide by which we walk, according to Paul in 2 Corinthians 5.7. Further, this faith comes by hearing the word of Christ (Romans 10.17).

Thus, seeking God's righteousness, like seeking God's kingdom, means looking for God's rule in our lives. It means searching His word and doing things His way.

Keep in mind that Jesus' statement in Matthew 6.33 was made in the context of the Sermon on the Mount. He had already said in Matthew 5.20, "For I say to you that unless your righteousness surpasses that of the scribes and Pharisees, you will not enter the kingdom of heaven." The Pharisees' righteousness was one of appearance and ritual (cf. Matthew 23.23–28). Seeking first God's kingdom and righteousness means more than punching our ticket once a week "at church." Our families must not take pride in appearance but in heart (2 Corinthians 5.12).

Remember the verse that is the basis of our study. Psalm 127.1 says, "Unless the Lord builds the house, they labor in vain who build it…" The Lord is building the house when those of us in the house are living His way all the time.

SEEK God's Kingdom and Righteousness

Imagine you overslept and had to rush out to work without eating. When you got to work, your boss moved up your project deadline so you had to work directly through lunch. The thought of taking a snack break was completely out of the question. Once you got off work you had to rush to pick up Junior and get him to Boy Scouts. While he was there, you had to pick up little Suzy and take her to softball practice. You and the kids finally get home. What is the first thought on your mind?

FOOD!

If you are like me, the first thing you will do is hit the fridge or the pantry. If you can't find any food, you will make a late night run to Sonic or call Papa John's. That is the same approach we must take with seeking God's kingdom and righteousness. Like the song we sing based on Psalm 42.1, "As the deer pants for the water brooks, so my soul pants for You, O God." That is how much we are to desire God's kingdom and righteousness in our families.

Jesus said we are to *seek* God's kingdom and righteousness. This implies we do not have the fullness of God's kingdom and righteousness yet. Our family has not completed its journey in Christ. We must keep growing, progressing and improving. Second, we must actually be looking for God's kingdom and righteousness. We will not stumble across it the way we might luckily stumble across a $20 bill someone dropped. Further, God's kingdom and righteousness take work. Seeking is active and purposeful, not passive and accidental. Our families will not fall into God's kingdom and righteousness the way we might fall into bed.

The question then is what are you and your family doing to actively seek God's kingdom and righteousness?

Seek FIRST God's Kingdom and Righteousness

Satan does not care if we seek God's kingdom and righteousness. He simply wants us to seek something else first. In fact, one of Satan's biggest ploys is to let us think we are doing a lot of righteous and faithful things. We "go to church." We do our Bible lessons. We are reading this book every day for crying out loud. What more could God want? He wants to be the Prime Mover in our families.

Seeking God's kingdom first is not about ordering our daily activities. It does not mean we do our spiritual stuff in the morning and then everything else later. I can easily see the Pharisees perusing the Law as the sun rose and standing on the street corners offering up their loud prayers before they headed to the market place to begin devouring the widows' houses (Matthew 23.14). That may be prioritizing spiritual activities, but it is not seeking God's kingdom and righteousness first. Seeking God's kingdom and righteousness first means God's rule is the motivating factor for everything we do.

Seeking God's kingdom and righteousness must be why you read your Bible and study it with your family. It is why you pray individually and together. It is why you work in the local congregation. It is why you go to work. It is why you love your wife, respect your husband, honor your parents and raise your children in the nurture and admonition of the Lord. It is even the motivation behind your periods of recreation and entertainment.

Interestingly, in 2 Corinthians 8.5, the Macedonians were able to give themselves to the Judeans and help them in their time of need, because they had first given themselves to God. When we give ourselves and our families to God first, we get all the other aspects of life right as well.

Don't Get Distracted

When Paul taught about receiving the righteousness which comes from God on the basis of faith he also wrote:

> *But whatever things were gain to me, those things I have counted as loss for the sake of Christ. More than that, I count all things to be loss in view of the surpassing value of knowing Christ Jesus my Lord, for whom I have suffered the loss of all things and count them but rubbish so that I may gain Christ (Philippians 3.7–8).*

For Paul, seeking God's kingdom and righteousness meant giving up a lot. It meant giving up his place of high standing among the Jewish nation and his ancestral traditions. Paul was willing to give all that up, because it would only distract from accomplishing his goal.

He continued in Philippians 3.11–14:

> *...in order that I may attain to the resurrection from the dead. Not that I have already obtained it or have already become perfect, but I press on so that I may lay hold of that for which also I was laid hold of by Christ Jesus. Brethren, I do not regard myself as having laid hold of it yet; but one thing I do: forgetting what lies behind and reaching forward to what lies ahead, I press on toward the goal for the prize of the upward call of God in Christ Jesus.*

Paul was heading for a goal and he would not let anything distract him. We must do the same.

In Matthew 6.31–32, Jesus provided the Gentiles' contrast to seeking first God's kingdom and righteousness, saying, "Do not worry then, saying, 'What will we eat?' or 'What will we drink?' or 'What will we wear for clothing?' For the Gentiles eagerly seek all these things; for your heavenly Father knows that you need all these things."

This becomes especially tough in the context of family. Perhaps if all we were concerned about was ourselves, this wouldn't be so bad. But our families? Our wives? Our husbands? Our kids? Are we really not to be primarily motivated by making sure our kids have food on the table and clothes for school? Certainly, we provide for our families. Those who do not are worse than infidels (1 Timothy 5.8). However, our primary motivation must never be about providing food and clothes, even for our children. Our primary motivation must be to serve God, seeking His kingdom and righteousness. That will include obeying 1 Timothy 5.8.

And All These Things Will Be Added To You

When God is the prime mover in our lives, He will provide all those other things that we need. After all, He knows what we need even before we ask (Matthew 6.8).

Further, our good Father in heaven is a giver of good gifts. "If you then being evil, know how to give good gifts to your children, how much more will your Father who is in heaven give what is good to those who ask Him!" (Matthew 7.11). He wants to bless us, not leave us hanging out to dry.

Remember Psalm 127.2, "It is vain for you to rise up early, to retire late, to eat the bread of painful labors; for He gives to His beloved even in his sleep." We may work all we want, but if we are distracted from seeking first God's kingdom and righteousness, our work is in vain. However, we may seek first God's kingdom and righteousness and wonder how God is going to feed us and clothe us. Never fear, He can bless us in our sleep.

Don't get caught up in the world's rat race. Seek first God's kingdom and righteousness and He will bless you with all you need.

Today's Response:

Consider Abraham's life, especially in view of Hebrews 11.8–19. How did Abraham seek first God's kingdom and righteousness and how did God bless Him?

What does this say about God's ability to bless you when you and your family seek first God's kingdom and righteousness?

Point to Ponder:

If someone on the outside were to take an objective look at your family, how it spends its time and money, what would they believe you are seeking first? What changes, if any, do you need to make based on your answer to the above question?

Today's Prayer:

Great and awesome God,

Yours is the kingdom, the power and the glory. Riches and honor come from You. It lies in Your hand to make great and to strengthen.

Grant my family strength to seek first Your kingdom and righteousness. Be the Prime Mover in our lives. Help us take the way of escape from sin and follow Your path at all times.

Help us keep our eyes on the prize and not be turned to the right or left by the devil's distractions. Please forgive us for the times we have been distracted from Your way.

We love you, Father.

By Your Son's authority we pray,

Amen

Week 1

4

Keeping the Family Together

The Great American Struggle

Family life in 21st Century America is not easy. Though, I imagine our New Testament counterparts would scoff at such a statement.

When we want to take a hot bath, we walk 10 feet into our bathroom and turn a couple of knobs. We do not have to take 15 trips to the river with two buckets and then light a fire to heat the water. If we want to cook a meal, we walk into the kitchen, put some food in a pan, turn some knobs on the oven and wait. Or, we pull something out of a freezer, shove it into a microwave, punch a few buttons and have a meal in five minutes. Or better yet, we hop in our air conditioned cars and drive ten minutes to a place where somebody else does the cooking for us. Few of us have to plow a field, plant and cultivate seed. Few of us have to raise cattle or hunt wild game. We do not have to chop down wood daily with which to cook our food. If we want to wear clothes, we drive to the store (again in our air conditioned cars) and buy some. We do not have to make thread, weave material and sew our own clothes. Then when those clothes are dirty, we sort them into piles of matching colors and dump them in machines that wash and dry them for us. We do not have to carry them down to the river, beat them on a rock, try to scrape the dirt and muck out of them and then hang them out to dry.

Let's face it. Our lives really are easy. What took our New Testament brethren hours to do takes us minutes, if we have to do it at all. This actually means we have more leisure time available than anyone in history. Don't close the book. I know what you are thinking. "Where does this nut get off saying I have all kinds of leisure time?" I am saying that because you and I do not have to spend most of every day just providing the bare necessities of life. We actually have enough time to work overtime and get paid time and a half. We actually have enough time to put our kids in little league, football, soccer, scouts and other activities. Our New Testament brethren did not have enough time for all the things that make our lives hectic because they spent their time surviving.

All this leisure time, however, has given us our own set of hardships. Few of us struggle for the necessities of life. However, because we have so much leisure time and so many opportunities to pursue pastimes, many of us struggle regarding the necessities of maintaining proper family relationships and togetherness.

Consider the following family.

Mom and Dad want to provide the best in housing, clothing and education for little Billy and Susie. Therefore they both work in the corporate world. They get up early to drop Billy and Susie at school. Billy and Susie are three years apart, so Dad carries Billy to middle school on his way to work and secretly thinks, "I sure am glad I am saving up enough money to buy Billy a car in a few years. When he turns sixteen he can take himself and Susie to school and I will have a little more time to myself." Mom drops Susie off at elementary school.

On Mondays, Wednesdays and Fridays, Billy has practice for the school play right after school. Then he has either little league or soccer after that. Mom or Dad rushes to pick up Susie from school, then goes to get Billy to take him from play practice to sports practice, then runs through the drive through to get something for the kids to eat. They let Susie eat in the car on the way to her Monday piano lessons and drop her off in time to pick Billy up from sports practice. He eats while they drive back to get Suzy. They hurry home to make the kids do their homework before shuffling them off to bed. Wednesdays are tough because they have to fit all this in before Bible class.

On Tuesdays and Thursdays, Billy has baseball games or soccer matches, while Susie has softball practice. All of Susie's softball games and tournaments are on the weekends. When the softball season is over, Susie's Saturdays are filled with tennis lessons and competitions. On Thursday, they also try to fit in scouts for both of the kids. Fortunately, the parents in each troop take turns picking up several of the kids from school and taking them to their various den and troop meetings.

Mom and Dad want to be active in Billy and Susie's schooling. They work with both PTAs (elementary and middle school). They try to make it to all the parent-teacher conferences. Billy is in the band and Susie is in the choir and they attend all of their concerts and competitions.

On top of all of this, Mom and Dad have lives of their own. They have to fit work into all this. Every once in a while they have to go on business trips. Further, they try to find time to pursue their personal hobbies. That is tough because of all the time they spend helping Billy and Susie with school projects.

Mom and Dad are Christians and they hope Billy and Susie will be someday too. It is very important to them to make it to all the worship services and Bible classes. They do make it to most of them. However, to be honest, it does rumple their feathers a little when the preacher comments on how few people are getting their lessons completed. "Doesn't he realize what an amazing feat it is for us to be here?" they wonder. They get to the building and shuffle the kids off to their classes and then go to theirs. They come into the worship assembly. The new preacher is big into getting all the kids to sit together, so the kids sit down on the front few rows away from their parents. The one making announcements talks about the training class for the boys taking place every Sunday afternoon, the Sunday night devotional for the middle school and high school, the Bible drill for the elementary kids and the various special things members have set up for the various age groups.

When the family does get a few minutes to be together on a Friday or Saturday evening, they are so exhausted they decide to simply pop in a video or go to the movies. They sit next to each other but are mentally miles apart as they gaze upon the silver screen.

In the extremely few moments of solitude and meditation, Mom and Dad wonder how they can fit anything else into their schedule and are about ready to murder the author of a book who claims they have more leisure time than anyone in history.

Does any of this sound familiar?

Is it any wonder even Christian families are falling apart? With these kinds of schedules, when were these families ever sticking together? Add into this equation that time at home is often spent just as separate as time at school, work and church. The family are all within the same dwelling, but each member is doing his or her own thing. Each child has their own room, equipped with television, telephone or computer (with internet access). They can spend all evening in the same house with two to four other people and never actually see each other.

This is the great American struggle—keeping the family together.

Meaningful Together Time

Let me make one thing perfectly clear. To my knowledge, there is nothing wrong with any of the activities mentioned in the previous section in and of themselves. The answer to the problem is not necessarily to end all extra-curricular activities (though some may take that approach). The point is, with so many opportunities waiting to take each family member away from the family unit, we have to be on our guard to preserve family togetherness.

There is only one way to do this. We must carve out and schedule meaningful family together time. Further, we must not buy into the modern mumbo-jumbo saying, "It's about quality time not quantity time." There is not a single person out there who can teach us how to prefab quality time into fifteen minute chunks no matter how many books you buy with questions to stimulate "meaningful" conversation. Quality time is the result of quantity time. There is no way around that.

Deuteronomy 6.7 provides some interesting insight to quality time. I recognize this passage talks about the Israelites passing the Law on to their children. We typically use this passage, rightly so, to discuss passing the gospel on to ours. However, let's look at it from a broader base. The verse says, "You shall teach them diligently to your sons and shall talk of them when you sit in your house and when you walk by the way and when you lie down and when you rise up."

These Israelites were able to have quality time, passing the Law to their children because they spent time sitting together in the house and walking together in the way. They had time together when they got up and before they went to bed. Do we take that kind of time together with our families?

We need to make time for the whole family to sit together in the house. Meal time is a great time for this. However, there ought to be other times as well. By time together, I do not mean time in the same house, but each in separate rooms. There needs to be time when all the televisions and computers are turned off, when all the phones are in the cradles and Mom, Dad and the kids are together.

Many of us wonder, "What on earth is there to do if we have turned off the tv and computers?" Read a book together and discuss what happens. Visit with one another the same way you would if you had company. Discuss what has happened in your individual lives that day. Ask each other for advice. Confide in each other. Play games together. A lot of life's lessons can be passed along over a game of Yahtzee or dominoes.

Let me encourage you to resist the urge to make all of your family time movie time. Watching television is always an individual activity no matter who you are sitting next to. Each person is individually interacting with what is on the screen. No one is interacting with each other. When you do have movie time as family time, make sure to discuss the movie together afterwards. What did you learn from it? What were your favorite parts? What were your least favorite? What did you think when so and so said such and such? And so on.

Of course, as Deuteronomy 6.7 directly states, you need to study God's word together and teach God's word. Look at the book of Proverbs. The whole book is a parent's recognition he has to teach his children. Do not think sermons and Bible classes are enough to teach your kids to be faithful Christians. They are not and God never intended them to be.

Along these same lines, the next time you go to a group Bible study, prayer time or singing, have your kids stay and be involved. Don't send them off to the play room, tacitly teaching them that spiritual things are too big for them. Even if they do not get to say anything or ask any questions, what a great opportunity your kids will have to hear adults discuss the Bible and how it impacts their lives.

One more opportunity for together time is working together. This is perhaps one of the biggest reasons we do not have time with family that our Bible counterparts had. Why did Mom and Dad have the ability to walk in the way with their children? They were going to the same places. When Mom was walking to the river with the clothes, little Susie was walking with her. When Dad was walking to the fields to plow, little Billy was walking with him.

We live in a different work culture. It is well nigh impossible to go back to that kind of work culture and I doubt any of us really want to. However, we need to figure out ways to work together as a family. Get the kids involved in yard work. Have them help you clean the house. Go together to someone who has a need and work together meeting the need. Visit the sick and shut-in together. Talk with each other as you walk in these ways. I guarantee you, the more of this time you spend together, the more quality moments you will rack up.

There is one more way the Old Testament demonstrated for producing family togetherness. In the Old Testament, we see memorials that set the Israelites apart as a group and prompted time to pass their faith along to their children. Consider passages like Exodus 12.25–27. God established an annual memorial to pass on Israel's identity as His special people. When the family observed the Passover together every year, the children would eventually ask about it. There was quality time that came out of quantity time.

Certainly, it is good for you to have memorials of spiritual significance. However, we can broaden this concept, realizing family traditions provide family togetherness prompting quality time and meaningful interaction. Those traditions, whether they surround holidays, birthdays or any other aspect of family life, will provide a marker, causing your family to identify with one another.

Family traditions do not have to be anything out of this world. I know one family whose tradition is what they call "worm cakes." It is essentially a bundt cake cut in half and pieced together to look like a worm. Then it is decorated with colored icing. Oreos are crushed up to provide dirt. It is given jelly bean or M & M eyes. They might lay gummy worms around it to be its friends. Sometimes they use licorice sticks to make hair. Each one is decorated differently. These cakes were used on birthdays, holidays, special events. Amazingly enough, these little cakes became so important, when this family's two sons got married, guess what kind of cake they wanted for their groom's cake. That's right—a worm cake. Not much, just a family tradition providing great memories and togetherness.

The Church and Family Togetherness

At this point we enter some muddy waters. The modern trend is for churches to provide activities for all the young people. Even if the activities are scriptural in nature, I begin to question the ultimate benefit of the church being overly involved in this.

Churches, instead of being another institution that separates the family into age categories, ought to do everything possible to get families together. We must remember the church is not supposed to take the place of the family.

Satan is working in our culture to rip our families to shreds. Churches must stand as shining beacons to overcome Satan in this by drawing families together in Christ. Perhaps we really should encourage kids to sit with their families in worship. Maybe we should try family-based Bible classes sometimes and not just age-segregated classes. Maybe we should teach fathers and mothers to train their children instead of just scheduling another training class at which parents are to drop off their kids. I am not sure all the ways this can be done, but I am sure we need to examine this.

Whatever the approach of the congregation, we must keep in mind our family has got to stay together. What are we doing to draw our families closer? In our culture this kind of togetherness does not happen accidentally. If we are not doing something to accomplish this on purpose, we are probably not going to accomplish it.

Today's Response:

What will you and your family do this week to have meaningful together time? Don't just write it down here. Schedule it and do it.

Point to Ponder:

What kind of teaching opportunities could the congregation offer to help keep the family together?

Today's Prayer:

Holy God,

We praise You for the family and Your wisdom in establishing it. Please strengthen our family. Help us draw close to one another as we draw close to you.

Father, help us not get so distracted with our own individual pursuits we neglect to keep our family together. Please forgive us for when we have been selfish in pursuing our own ends.

Thank You Lord for Your love and help us love our families as You do. We love you, Father.

By Your Son's authority we pray,

Amen

Family First

Which Is It?

Alright, I admit it. I chose the above title for the alliteration. "Family Second" just wouldn't have the same ring to it. I don't want you to be confused. I am not going to contradict the earlier chapter which clearly points out we must seek God's kingdom and righteousness first.

Rather, the very first place and the very first relationship in which God wants us to seek first His kingdom and righteousness is in the family relationship. The very first place in which we need to make sure we are obeying God and doing things His way is in our homes.

Additionally, we need to recognize God has placed a priority on our families. As we are seeking opportunities to serve and glorify God, the place we need to start is in our family. Do not be overcome thinking you are only truly serving God if you go off into some foreign land and evangelize the natives. You need to start at home.

In Mark 5, after Jesus cast out "Legion" from the man of the Gerasenes, he wanted to accompany Jesus. He was willing to leave his home and family in order to follow the Lord. However, Jesus said in vs. 19, "Go home to your people and report to them what great things the Lord has done for you, and how He had mercy on you."

Look at Andrew. He ended up being an apostle. But where did he start? In John 1.40–41, Andrew first went to his brother Simon Peter. Family is where we need to start as well.

Family before Self

In Genesis 2.24, Moses wrote, "For this reason a man shall leave his father and mother, and be joined to his wife; and they shall become one flesh." Before marriage, an individual is exactly that—an individual. In general, that person is free to live however they choose (so long as they are obeying God). The individual can live where he wants. She can have whatever job she chooses. He can come and go as he pleases. She can pursue whatever goals she desires.

However, when two individuals marry, they lose their individuality. Sadly, too many married people are upset if they are known as so-and-so's husband or so-and-so's wife. Most people, though married, still want to be individuals who are not known for their family but for themselves. However, family should come before self.

1 Corinthians 7.32–34 says:

> *But I want you to be free from concern. One who is unmarried is concerned about the things of the Lord, how he may please the Lord; but one who is married is concerned about the things of the world, how he may please his wife, and his interests are divided. The woman who is unmarried, and the virgin, is concerned about the things of the Lord, that she may be holy both in body and spirit; but one who is married is concerned about the things of the world, how she may please her husband.*

Before marriage, our interests are solely focused on how we can serve the Lord and be holy as individuals. Once we become married, part of our serving the Lord is being concerned about pleasing our spouse (by extension, being concerned about pleasing our children when they come along).

In this context, Paul was afraid the concern for family would cause some not to serve the Lord. The point we are noticing is simply that once we are married we must be concerned about pleasing our spouse. Family comes before self.

Family before Career

1 Timothy 5.8 says, "But if anyone does not provide for his own, and especially for those of his household, he has denied the faith and is worse than an unbeliever." Prior to that in vss. 3–4, Paul wrote, "Honor widows who are widows indeed; but if any widow has children or grandchildren, they must first learn to practice piety in regard to their own family and to make some return to their parents; for this is acceptable in the sight of God."

Ephesians 4.28 says, "He who steals must steal no longer; but rather he must labor, performing with his own hands what is good, so that he will have something to share with one who has need."

We must understand the place of our jobs in the big picture. When we stand before the judgment seat of God, He is not going to ask what kind of job we had. He is not going to ask how much money we made. He is not going to ask how powerful or influential we were in the business community. He is going to want to know if we used the blessings He gave us through our careers to be a blessing to others. Were we a blessing to our families?

This is a tough issue to talk about. I am afraid many of us have deceived ourselves. Too many put their career before everything and justify it by saying they are trying to provide for their family. It is right to work hard. It is ok to work a job that pays well. It is ok to even enjoy luxuries when God has blessed us abundantly (cf. Ecclesiastes 5.18–20). However, we must understand that providing for our family is not just about money, food, clothes and financial opportunities.

If our pursuit of career leaves us little time with our family, we must not deceive ourselves. If it leaves us unable to train our children up in the Lord, we must not deceive ourselves. If it leaves us unable to nurture and cherish our wives or love and respect our husbands, we must not deceive ourselves.

The long and short of it is this, you may have a wonderful job and a great career. It may be catapulting you to wealth, influence and fame. There is nothing wrong with any of those things. If God has blessed you in this way, give thanks. However, remember God has blessed you in this way to be a blessing to others, primarily your family. If at any point your career stops you from being a blessing to your family, you have left the Lord's straight and narrow path.

Family and God

Obviously, there is no sense in which family should come before God. Matthew 10.37 puts an end to that kind of thinking—"He who loves father or mother more than Me is not worthy of Me; and he who loves son or daughter more than Me is not worthy of Me."

However, we need to remember putting God first in our lives means placing a priority on our family. We are not allowed to use serving God as an excuse for not dealing with our family properly. The Pharisees made this mistake and were rebuked in Matthew 15.3–6.

> *And He answered and said to them, "Why do you yourselves transgress the commandment of God for the sake of your tradition? For God said, 'Honor your father and mother,' and, 'He who speaks evil of father or mother is to be put to death.' But you say, 'Whoever says to his father or mother, "Whatever I have that would help you has been given to God," he is not to honor his father or mother.' And by this you invalidated the word of God for the sake of your tradition."*

In Leviticus 27, God regulated devoting material possessions to God. He spoke of devoting animals, houses and fields. Apparently, the Pharisees had latched onto this passage and used it as a means not to provide for their families. "I can't use the produce of this field to support you; it has been devoted to the Lord."

Jesus said this did not wash with God. We cannot use supposed service to God as a means to deny provision for our family—whether financially, emotionally, mentally or spiritually. Anybody can get caught in this trap, but those with special roles have to be very careful. I know as a preacher how easy it is to spend so much time at the office, visiting the sick and shut-in, beating the bushes to set up Bible studies, making it to every event any brother or sister plans and not providing for the family as I ought. The preacher (or other worker) feels guilty thinking the choice is between the family and the Lord. The wife is afraid to complain because she thinks she will look selfish and unspiritual. The kids grow up mad at God for stealing their father. God did not have this in mind. Even the preacher's first work of counsel, evangelism and good deeds is his family.

I knew a family who was very dedicated to the work of the local congregation. The father was a deacon. If I remember correctly, he was the church's treasurer. Additionally, he and his wife were leaders regarding the Bible class program for the church's children. They spent a lot of time preparing curriculum, training teachers, decorating class rooms and covering for other workers who did not get their jobs done. Everything looked good on the outside, but at home, they were getting disconnected. Patience was thin, tempers flared often. The family was constantly walking on eggshells. What was worse, they were mad at God and the local congregation because they knew exactly what the source of the frustration was. They finally realized this was not a choice between God and their family. This was a choice between serving God properly by keeping the home safe and secure or putting up a show of serving God by doing more than anyone else in "church work." They chose to back off on "church work." Regrettably, they took some heat from some for not being spiritual enough. I think they made the right choice.

Do not misunderstand, I am not saying wait until your kids are grown to get involved in "church work." I am not saying fill your schedule with secular extra-curriculars and only do work in the local congregation if you just happen to end up with some extra time. I am simply saying we need to maintain balance regarding home responsibilities and congregational responsibilities—no matter what our role in the local congregation.

Prioritize Family

Stephen Covey, author of *The Seven Habits of Highly Effective People,* tells the story of a professor conducting a lecture about time management who stood before his class with a big bucket. He filled the bucket with big rocks and asked the class, "Is it full?" The class said, "Yes." But then he pulled out some smaller rocks from under the table and began to shake them down in between the big rocks. When he could get no more little rocks in the bucket, he asked, "Is it full?" The class said, "Yes." But then the professor pulled out some sand and shook the sand down through the big and little rocks, until he could put no more sand in. He asked the class, "Is it full now?" The class had caught on and said nothing. He then pulled out a container of water and poured in the water until it was brimming at the top. At this point, all agreed it was full.

Then the professor asked, "What was the point of this illustration?" One brave soul responded, "You have demonstrated that we always have time to do more if we fill in the little spaces." "Wrong," said the professor. "I have just demonstrated that if I hadn't put the big rocks in first, I would not have had room for them."

Remember that. In God's book your family is a big rock. Prioritize it. Place it in the bucket of your life first and don't let all the other distractions take you away from it.

Today's Response:

In your family, ask each other what the others think is most important in your life? Let each other be honest and don't get defensive. If serving God and serving your family are not high on their list for you, discuss how to improve it.

Point to Ponder:

Consider the roles in each of your lives and how you can all have balance in your family lives, working together to help each other keep family first.

Today's Prayer:

Heavenly Father,

We praise Your name. Please abide with us, strengthening us to please and provide for the family You have given us.

Help us not be distracted by other pursuits. Help us use the blessings You have given us to be a blessing to others, especially our family.

God strengthen us to be Your servants by serving our families above ourselves and our careers. Thank You for our family

We love You Father.

Through Your Son we pray,

Amen

Week One Group Discussion

- What are the most important lessons you have learned this week?

- What questions do you have about what you learned this week?

- What practical improvement have you and your family made in your family lives based on what you learned this week?

- What practical advice would you give others to accomplish what you learned this week?

- With what issues do you and your family need help or prayers based on what you learned this week?

- How can a family make sure they are seeking first God's kingdom and righteousness?

- What advice would you give other families to help them spend meaningful time together and keep the family first?

Week Two:
Family Goals

"Not that I have already obtained it or have already become perfect, but I press on so that I may lay hold of that for which also I was laid hold of by Christ Jesus. Brethren, I do not regard myself as having laid hold of it yet; but one thing I do: forgetting what lies behind and reaching forward to what lies ahead, I press on toward the goal for the prize of the upward call of God in Christ Jesus."

Philippians 3.12–14

Week 2

6

The Ultimate Goal: Heaven

Does Anything Else Matter?

A young man was bragging about his upcoming graduation from high school with honors. A wise older man asked him, "What do you plan to do after graduation."

"I'm going to college."

"And after that?"

"I will get a job."

"And after that?"

"I'm going to make lots of money and be rich. I'm going to get married and raise a family."

"And after that?"

"I'm going to retire and enjoy the high life. Spend time with my grandkids. Travel the world and enjoy my old age."

"And after that?"

"Well, I guess by that time I will be ready to die."

"And after that?"

*****

Another man was bragging about how productive his land had been and all the crops he had to store up. "What shall I do next?" he asked himself.

"I will build big huge barns, store all my goods and live off them for the rest of my life, taking my ease, eating, drinking and being merry."

But then God said to him in Luke 12.20, "You fool! This very night your soul is required of you; and now who will own what you have prepared?"

*****

In Philippians 3.13–14, Paul wrote, "Brethren, I do not regard myself as having laid hold of it yet; but one thing I do: forgetting what lies behind and reaching forward to what lies ahead, I press on toward the goal for the prize of the upward call of God in Christ Jesus."

This is the ultimate goal—heaven. It is the most important goal. It is, in fact, the only important goal. Think about it. Is there anything in life that you would accomplish and say, "You know what? Since I accomplished this goal, spending eternity in hell will be worth it"?

In like manner, is there anything in life that you would accomplish and say, "You know what? Since I accomplished this goal, letting my spouse, parents or kids spend eternity in hell will be worth it"?

There will come a day when we will not care what kind of job we had. We will not care if our spouse made lots of money. We will not care what kind of house we lived in or car we drove. We will not care what school our kids went to. We will not care if they ever played baseball, softball, football or volleyball. We will not care if our kids made the honor roll. We will not care about whether or not we owned a computer, a boat, a vacation home or anything else. We will only care about one thing. Are we going to heaven?

We must understand, however, the decision regarding whether we will go to heaven or hell will not be made on that day of judgment. It is being made right now based on how we choose to live.

Therefore, in your family, whether you are the husband or wife, parent or child, brother or sister, you must realize there is only one goal for you—getting to heaven and helping your family get there too. One day, that will be all that matters. Why not make that day today?

Running the Race

Paul described our spiritual journey as a race saying:

> *Do you not know that those who run in a race all run, but only one receives the prize? Run in such a way that you may win. Everyone who competes in the games exercises self-control in all things. They then do it to receive a perishable wreath, but we an imperishable. Therefore I run in such a way, as not without aim; I box in such a way, as not beating the air; but I discipline my body and make it my slave, so that, after I have preached to others, I myself will not be disqualified (1 Corinthians 9.24–27).*

We need to view our walk in Christ together as a family as though we are running a marathon. If we want to win the prize, we have to train properly.

First, we must exercise. Hebrews 5.14 says, "But solid food is for the mature, who because of practice have their senses trained to discern good and evil." Through study and application of scripture, we train our senses to discern between good and evil and thus learn to exercise self-control as Paul encouraged in 1 Corinthians 9.24–27.

I have been a runner off and on for several years. Recently, I have started getting my kids involved in the running. They are at different levels but it is exciting to see them develop disciplines of exercise at an early age. Perhaps you are doing something with your kids to teach them to exercise. The question for both of us is what are we doing to exercise our families in the Word of God, helping them learn to exercise self-control?

Second, we have to do this on purpose. Paul said he did not run in such a way as to run without aim or box in such a way as beating the air. That is, he did things on purpose. He understood he would not win the prize on accident. He had to have a plan and he had to pursue his goal consciously.

What plan do you have to get your family to heaven? Do you think you can just get them to church pretty regularly and that ought to cover it? I wouldn't bank on that.

Third, Paul said he had to discipline his body and bring it into subjection. He could not just do anything he wanted. He had to give up some things. That is not easy, but it is necessary. In Philippians 3.7, he wrote, "Whatever things were gain to me, those things I have counted as loss for the sake of Christ."

There are many things we can see as positives in this life. There are many good things we can pursue. But if these distract us from the best pursuit, we need to get rid of them. Consider Mary and Martha in Luke 10.38–42. Martha was busy with preparations for a meal and for hospitality. There was nothing wrong with that in and of itself. It was good, and there would be a time for it. However at that moment, Jesus' teaching was what would help her accomplish the ultimate goal. Mary chose that good part and it would not be taken away from her.

Reaching Forward

In Philippians 3.12–14, Paul explained he was pressing on for the prize. Two aspects of his statement are important to note here.

First, he pressed on because he realized he had not attained the goal. I am really concerned about all the people who so bank on God's grace they act as though there is nothing more required of them. They already "got saved." Paul said he had not attained the goal. He would press on.

Our families have not attained the goal. No matter what we have done or accomplished, we are not in heaven yet. We must keep working. We must keep growing. We must keep pressing on.

Second, he forgot what went behind. Paul put failures and successes alike in the past. He would not allow past failures to cause him to quit running the race. Nor would he allow past successes to make him think he did not have to run quite as hard today.

Like any race, we will have ups and downs. We cannot allow these ups and downs to turn our head from the prize. We have to put those ups and downs behind us, look ahead and keep putting one foot in front of the other.

This is one of the reasons running this race together as a family is so important. As the Preacher said in Ecclesiastes 4.9–12:

> *Two are better than one because they have a good return for their labor. For if either of them falls, the one will lift up his companion. But woe to the one who falls when there is not another to lift him up. Furthermore, if two lie down together they keep warm, but how can one be warm alone? And if one can overpower him who is alone, two can resist him. A cord of three strands is not quickly torn apart.*

Redeem the Time

One final aspect of this is that we do not know how long we have to run this race. Perhaps if we knew we, our spouses, our parents and our kids were going to live for another 5, 10, 25, 50 years we could put off running this race. It would be harder to get started, but we could do it. The problem is we don't know that.

Paul said, "Therefore be careful how you walk, not as unwise men but as wise, making the most of your time, because the days are evil" (Ephesians 5.15–16). When he said the days are evil, I believe he was alluding to Ecclesiastes 9.12 where the Preacher said, "Moreover, man does not know his time: like a fish caught in a treacherous net and birds trapped in a snare, so the sons of men are ensnared at an evil time when it suddenly falls on them."

We never know what a day will bring. As I write this, I am thinking about a conversation I had with a brother in Christ just last night. He told me of a recently graduated high school senior who played ball with my friend's son. This young man had a promising future as far as the world is concerned. He looked like an eventual shoe-in for the pros. However, just a few days ago, he was riding in the bed of a truck. The driver swerved for some reason and the young man was thrown from the back of the truck and killed. Who knew? The days are evil. Right now, it doesn't matter how good of a ball player that young man was. What matters is whether or not he had been growing in Christ?

We have no idea what today, tomorrow or the next day will bring for you or your family. We must not put off working toward the ultimate goal. Today may be the last day we have to go in that direction.

We must look at everything our family does from the standpoint of how we will feel about it on the Day of Judgment. If we live each day with that in mind, then the ultimate goal will be ours. Let's call our family together, put our running shoes on and press on for the prize today. If we see tomorrow, do it again. It is running. It is not easy. It will be a struggle sometimes. But believe me, for all that it might cost us today or tomorrow, there will come a day when we will know it was worth it all. As Paul said in Romans 8.18, "For I consider that the sufferings of this present time are not worthy to be compared with the glory that is to be revealed to us."

Today's Response:

What is your plan for the next several years to get your family to heaven?

What is your plan for today and tomorrow to redeem the time and help your family reach forward for the prize, considering these might be your last days?

Point to Ponder:

Are there any pursuits that are distracting you and your family from pressing on for the prize in Christ Jesus? If so, what are they and how can you overcome them?

Today's Prayer:

Glorious God,

Thank You for Your Son whose blood washes our sins away allowing us the hope of heaven. Help us pursue that goal with all our might.

Keep us safe from the tempter's snares. Help us not be deceived by his deluding influence.

Father, give us the strength to sacrifice what hinders our race with You and please forgive us for when we have failed. Lift us up and help us continue on. Please, receive us into Your dwelling place in the end.

We love You Father.

Through Your Son we pray,

Amen

Our Spiritual Goal: Bearing Fruit to God's Glory

A Family of Disciples

A lot of parents make it their goal to get their kids baptized. That, however, is not enough. Retention rate for kids remaining faithful to the Lord once they leave home seems to be sadly low. Regrettably, I have been unable to discover any hard and fast statistics. Anecdotally, however, the older brethren who have paid attention over the years claim anywhere from 50 to 80% leave the faith when they leave the home.

How do we overcome this? Obviously, there is no certain way to raise faithful Christians. Our kids will eventually make their own choices. Can we stack the deck in God's favor? I believe we can. However, it will not happen by working on getting our kids baptized, but on having a family of disciples.

In John 15.8, Jesus said, "My Father is glorified by this, that you bear much fruit and so prove to be My disciples." This should be the spiritual goal of every family, of every Christian. Or, to borrow modern business lingo, this should be our mission.

To God Be the Glory

Psalm 115 begins, "Not to us, O Lord, not to us but to Your name give glory." To develop a family of disciples, this has to be our priority. Instead of seeking our own glory through business, sports, fame, finances or whatever else, we need to seek God's glory.

The starting place for this is through family worship. We will devote an entire chapter to this concept later. For now, we must simply notice the importance of glorifying God through family worship.

Sadly, many Christian families spend no more time worshipping God than the time they spend with the local congregation. Even sadder, some families do not even take every opportunity available to glorify God with the congregation.

How much time does your family spend reading and studying the Bible together? How much time do you spend praying? How much time do you spend singing praises together? We make sure our kids get to school five days a week. We make sure they make it to their sports practices and games several days a week. How much more important is it to make sure they worship God every day?

Is God being glorified in your family through constant and continual worship? Consider Psalm 115.12–15 and the blessings that come to those who fear, honor, trust and glorify the Lord:

> *The Lord has been mindful of us; He will bless us;*
> *He will bless the house of Israel;*
> *He will bless the house of Aaron.*
> *He will bless those who fear the Lord,*
> *The small together with the great.*
> *May the Lord give you increase,*
> *You and your children.*
> *May you be blessed of the Lord,*
> *Maker of heaven and earth.*

Blessing comes when our goal is to glorify God.

Sowing in the Family Garden

Jesus often taught in parables. One of His most famous is the Parable of the Sower, found in Matthew 13.3–9.

> *"Behold, the sower went out to sow; and as he sowed, some seeds fell beside the road, and the birds came and ate them up. Others fell on the rocky places, where they did not have much soil; and immediately they sprang up, because they had no depth of soil. But when the sun had risen, they were scorched; and because they had no root, they withered away. Others fell among the thorns, and the thorns came up and choked them out. And others fell on the good soul and yielded a crop, some a hundredfold, some sixty, and some thirty. He who has ears to hear, let him hear."*

We typically view this as a parable about evangelism (because it is). How often, though, do we apply it to our family life? This parable is really about being a fruit bearing Christian. It is, therefore, about how to glorify the Father and prove ourselves His disciples.

From Matthew 13.18–23, we know that the seed on the roadside, eaten by the birds represents those who hear the word, but have it removed by the evil one. We don't want this kind of soil in our family heart. Therefore, we need to remove as much of the influence of the evil one as possible. That means monitoring television, radio, movies, magazines and books. Further, it means keeping up a constant and continual sowing of the seed. Granted, we can't shove the Bible down anyone's throat, not even our family's. However, we can make the Bible, the worship of God and the life of Christ a constant anchor in our family. If we do that, we will develop a "worldview" for our children and ourselves that will not be easily taken away. As Proverbs 22.6 says, "Train up a child in the way he should go, even when he is old he will not depart from it."

The seed on rocky places represents the one who has heard and accepted, but is unable to put out many roots. Things look fine for a while but when the sun rises and the heat increases, their faith is fried. This describes far too many children who enter the heat of the sun under the withering gaze of a humanist professor or the caustic taunts of immoral peers. Like the good gardener, we have to remove the rocks if we expect spirituality to grow. We must not be satisfied with an eventual baptism in children or adults. We must then begin to work on deep roots in the word of God. Psalm 119.11 says, "Your word I have treasured in my heart, that I may not sin against you." We have to get that word into the heart of our family. The problem is, as we have discussed in previous chapters, we have so little time. We have so many rocks in our garden, it is hard to get those roots growing. We have to get rid of the rocks. Do you remember Jesus' statement in Matthew 5.29–30.

> *If your right eye makes you stumble, tear it out and throw it from you; … If your right hand makes you stumble, cut it off and throw it from you; for it is better for you to lose one of the parts of your body, than for your whole body to go into hell.*

If extra-curricular activities are stealing your time to plant the word of God in your heart and in your family's heart, then get rid of them. As we learned in the last chapter, a day will come when you will not care how many extra activities you were able to experience.

The seed sown among the weeds represents those who hear the word and believe it. However, in time, the worries, pleasures and riches of the world choke out the word. This is a matter of priorities. Our families can tell what the biggest priority in our homes is. If they see the biggest priority is keeping up with the neighbors, expect them to worry about appearances. If they see the biggest priority is wealth, expect them to worry about money. If they see the biggest priority is glorifying God, they will be able to keep the rest in balance. Further, the entire family needs to learn to rely on God. As Paul taught in Philippians 4.6, "Be anxious for nothing, but in everything by prayer and supplication with thanksgiving let your requests be made known to God." If this principle governs our families, we have automatically weeded our family garden.

The final seed sown on good soil is where we all want to be. This seed represents the good heart, in which the word digs deep roots and grows tall bearing a great amount of fruit. Some will bear thirtyfold, some sixty and some a hundred, but all will bear fruit. God will be glorified and we will be proven Jesus' disciples.

God Glorifying Fruit

What fruit are we to bear in our family of disciples? Galatians 5.22–23 explains. "But the fruit of the Spirit is love, joy, peace, patience, kindness, goodness, faithfulness, gentleness and self-control..."

A full look at each of these Christian virtues would take a whole book of its own. Suffice it to say these are the characteristics we ought to be working on in our families.

Notice what is not in this list. The fruit of the Spirit is not genius, agility, speed or good looks. I remember a time when a good Christian family was being criticized because of some of the decisions they made regarding their children. The well-meaning parent who thought this family was short-changing their kids said something along the lines of, "I am not saying they can't teach their kids how they want, but at least my kids are going to know how to hit a baseball." He had recently witnessed a pitiful performance in a softball game by these kids when the people from his church had gotten together for a picnic and some fun and games. In our society, it seems like short-changing our family if they are not trained up in sports. When we watch somebody who can't hold the bat properly, can't catch a football or aim a kick at a soccer ball, we think they are just plain losers. But keep in mind, as we stand before God in judgment He won't be throwing us footballs. He will be examining the fruit in our garden.

Don't get me wrong. I love sports. I played them from age six up through college. I think some great lessons can come from organized sports. I just want to illustrate how we sometimes get confused about what really matters in life. Before we spend time working on a fastball, let's make sure we are developing love, joy, peace, patience, kindness, goodness, faithfulness, gentleness and self-control.

When we work on our family fruit garden, then we are proving to be Christ's disciples. Then we are glorifying God. Then we are accomplishing God's goal for our family.

Today's Response:

Pick one of the fruit of the Spirit from **Galatians 5.22–23**. How can you and your family purposefully work on that particular fruit for the next week? (Make plans to choose one per week for the next two months. You might like this enough to repeat it).

Point to Ponder:

Are there any rocks and weeds still in your personal and/or family garden? How can you and your family remove them together?

Today's Prayer:

Heavenly Father,

We thank You for Your Word and the life-giving message it contains. Help us treasure it in our hearts that we might overcome the tempter and glorify You.

Forgive us for the rocks and weeds we have allowed in our garden and strengthen us to clean them out.

Strengthen us to bear the fruit of Your Spirit in our individual lives and in our family. Help us maintain the proper focus every day, bearing fruit that glorifies You.

We love You Father.

Through Your Son we pray,

Amen

Relationship Goal #1: Love

What's Forever For?

If you are married you may remember the day you got dressed up, stood in front of a preacher and a big room full of people and vowed your life away to your spouse. If you are not married, you have probably at least witnessed that happen to someone else.

Do you remember the vows? If they were modeled after the traditional wedding vows, they went something like this:

> I, ________, take you ________, to be my wife (husband), to have and to hold, for better, for worse, for richer, for poorer, in sickness and in health, to love and to cherish; from this day forward until death do us part.

When we stated those vows, the idea of loving that person forever seemed easy. We had spent time together, talking endlessly and thought we had gotten to know our soon-to-be spouse. We couldn't imagine not loving them. The love we had in that moment, and the love we expected to maintain forever, was not really the Bible love. Further, that kind of love never lasts forever.

That love is more of an infatuation. We had a huge emotional connection to a picture of the person we had married. Then we came home from the honeymoon and found out our new husband or wife was actually a pain sometimes. They either are too flighty or they are too rigid. Your spouse may never plan anything (their irresponsibility just drives you nuts). Or they may not sneeze without marking it off their to-do list (such strict rigidness is absolutely annoying to you).

Perhaps your spouse is a bit of a slob, leaving dirty clothes in piles, half-empty milk glasses and coffee cups all over the house and never putting the cap back on the toothpaste. Why can't they see how degrading and trashy that is? On the other hand, your spouse may label their socks, put their outfits on color coded hangers and put your half-full coffee cup in the dishwasher because you set it down for a few minutes to make a phone call. Surely anyone can see this is over the top obsessive-compulsive behavior.

You got home from the honeymoon and expected your spouse to get to work on a million projects to provide for the family, fix-up the house or move up the corporate ladder. Instead, they just wanted to take a nap and get to work in a few hours. On the other hand, you may have wanted to spend a little time in intimate conversation, letting your hair down and just having together time. Regrettably, your spouse had too many irons in the fire to give you the time of day. They put on their work clothes, gave a quick kiss, muttered an "I love you" and headed out the door.

Does any of this sound familiar to you? After a few months of this, your prince charming has fallen from his white steed and your beauty queen is beginning to look a little rough around the edges. That love you thought was so strong it could never die began to diminish.

Enter children, stage left. They are so cute and cuddly, you knew full well you could never love anybody anymore than you did that kid.

But then those cute and cuddly children learned to talk back. They started breaking rules. They started running you ragged with their questions and requests: "Can I have…?" "Why …?" "But you said…?" And the one that just sends you over the edge when it comes only 30 minutes after a lunch they picked at and played with but hardly ate—"I'm hungry. How long 'til supper?"

We kids were once absolutely enthralled with mom and dad, nobody had better parents than us. But then mom and dad turned into these old fashioned out-dated eyesores who obviously do not know how the world really works. Their rules and restrictions cramp our lifestyles, not to mention the clothes they wore and the music they listen to. As the Fresh Prince anthemed back in the 80's, "Parents just don't understand." (Can you tell when I went through this phase? By the way, now that I am a parent, you are not actually allowed to listen to that song I just referenced from my teenage angst.)

What at one time seemed so easy to do inevitably hits a road block of seeming impossibility. But the vow is still there. Love is still the goal. Let me warn you, it will not happen overnight. It is a major growth process. It takes absolute purposeful discipline to love your family. It is something you need to work on together. However, you need to remember this, God never commanded you to make your family love you. He only commanded you to love your family forever.

How Do You Know When It's Love?

If you are talking about the infatuated teenager puppy-love, it is love when you get those butterflies in the pit of your stomach every time the person comes into the room. But as we said above, that love won't last.

If you are talking about the biblical concept of love that you are supposed to have, then look at 1 Corinthians 13.4–7. By the way, this passage is not talking about romantic love. This is the same love we are supposed to have for all people. However, if we can't develop this love with the man or woman we committed our lives to, the parents who raised us and the children we brought into the world, how can we expect to ever develop it for anyone else? You know it is love when it looks like this:

> *Love is patient, love is kind and is not jealous; love does not brag and is not arrogant, does not act unbecomingly; it does not seek its own, is not provoked, does not take into account a wrong suffered, does not rejoice in unrighteousness, but rejoices with the truth; bears all things, believes all things, hopes all things, endures all things.*

Just take a look at that list again. That is pretty extensive. It says it is not enough to think we can act however we want and then try to cover it up with an "I love you" and a nice birthday gift.

Too often we look at this list and think about how far short of it our spouse, parents or kids fall. Please remember Matthew 7.1–2. The standard with which you judge your family is the standard with which God will judge you. In other words, before you spend your time blasting your spouse about their lack of patience, their self-centeredness, etc., you had better look at yourself.

Love is patient. Love realizes our spouses are not perfect and need to grow. It knows children are not raised overnight. We must keep in mind God's patience with us. We sinned several times today, but God did not zap us. Instead, He has granted us time to grow and repent again and again (cf. 2 Peter 3.9).

Love is kind. Perhaps the best definition of kindness is found in Ephesians 4.29–32.

> *Let no unwholesome word proceed from your mouth, but only such a word as is good for edification according to the need of the moment, so that it will give grace to those who hear...Let all bitterness and wrath and anger and clamor and slander be put away from you, along with all malice. Be kind to one another, tender-hearted, forgiving each other, just as God in Christ also has forgiven you.*

How do we speak to our family? Does it provide grace to them? That is, are our words a gift to them, building them up? What about how we treat them? Are we tender-hearted and forgiving with them? A great goal for us is to perform at least one specific act of kindness for each family member every day.

Love is not jealous, does not brag and is not arrogant. These statements all go together presenting different aspects of the same issue—competition. Too often the family is the hottest bed of competition that exists, especially in our modern era of gender competition. God did not give men and women to each other to compete, but to complement. Our spouses are different from us. Not only that, our parents and children are different. Our siblings are different. Instead of competing with each other, jealously defending our superiority, complement each other. If our spouses, parents, children, brothers or sisters are strong in some area where we are weak, we should learn to rely on their strength to make us better. If they are weak in an area where we are strong, we must not hold it over their heads. Instead, give them a helping hand. Ecclesiastes 4.9–12 talks about the great value of teamwork. Our family should be a team that works together.

Love does not act unbecomingly. Love behaves appropriately. That is, love does not do anything that will bring itself or the object of love into disgrace. The standard of disgrace is, of course, God's standard, not the world's. I cannot help but think about one of the greatest travesties of our age—sexual abuse. Sadly, this happens more within the family than anywhere else. This is not the forum to get explicit. However, we need to remember that morality and purity are the standard for Christian conduct. Ephesians 5.3–13 provides some great guidelines for appropriate behavior.

> *But immorality or any impurity or greed must not even be named among you...and there must be no filthiness and silly talk, or coarse jesting, which are not fitting...Let no one deceive you with empty words, for because of these things the wrath of God comes upon the sons of disobedience. Therefore do not be partakers with them; for you were formerly darkness, but now you are Light in the Lord...do not participate in the unfruitful deeds of darkness, but instead even expose them; for it is disgraceful even to speak of these things which are done by them in secret.*

Love does not seek its own. Would you like to know the one Bible passage that is the key to success in marriage and other family relationships? We will have happy, healthy relationships with our spouses, parents, children and siblings to the degree that we follow this one passage. The passage is Philippians 2.3–4.

> *Do nothing from selfishness or empty conceit, but with humility of mind regard one another as more important than yourselves; do not merely look out for your own personal interests, but also for the interests of others.*

I cannot tell you how many times I have advised couples in turmoil to follow this verse. Almost inevitably, the next call will be from the husband or wife telling me how hard they tried, but it just didn't work because their spouse is still being a jerk. They just don't know how long they can go on. What they have just admitted is they really weren't following the verse. They were seeking their own, they were being manipulative. They tried for a time to be nice to their spouse, but they were only trying to get the spouse to be nice to them. They were not seeking benefit for their spouse for their spouse's sake. They were really seeking their personal benefit. Love does not seek its own.

Love is not provoked. Wow! This one is tough. How often do we allow ourselves to get blazing hot mad with our kids, our parents or our spouse? Amazingly, the relationships we claim are most based on love are the ones that most often violate this principle. Regrettably, we often take family relationships for granted. We assume they will always be there so we blow up, seethe, yell, reply sarcastically and hatefully. We would never talk that way to our boss, she would fire us. We would never talk that way to our employee, he would sue us. We would never talk that way to our neighbors. But we will talk that way to our family. We can say, "I love you" all day long, but we know it is love when we learn to control our anger and not be easily provoked.

Love does not take into account a wrong suffered. Let's face it, our family is not perfect. They are going to hurt us some times. In fact, the hurt that comes from family will be deeper than any other because we are so emotionally vulnerable in our family relationships. Love, however, does not keep score. Love overlooks the past. As Proverbs 10.12 says, "Hatred stirs up strife, but love covers all transgressions."

Love does not rejoice with unrighteousness, but rejoices with the truth. Love is not blind to sin. Love is not happy when the object of love is losing their soul through unrighteousness. Love will not go along with the pleasure caused by sinfulness. Further, it will call the sinner to account (gently, of course—Galatians 6.1). However, love does rejoice with truth and righteousness. Keep in mind this juxtaposition. Too many of us are quick to call our spouse, children or parents on the carpet when they are doing something wrong, but how often do we roll out the red carpet when they are doing something right. Righteousness and truth are reasons for rejoicing. Catch your family (especially your children) doing something right and rejoice with them for it.

Love bears all things, believes all things, hopes all things, endures all things. This is perhaps the ultimate. Love continues on whatever the circumstances. This love is unconditional. We do not love just as long as we are loved. We do not love just when life is easy. Remember those vows? "For better, for worse, for richer, for poorer, in sickness and in health 'til death parts us." Too many people are willing to go only so far in this vow. They didn't realize their vow meant to love and cherish when things are this bad, when they are this poor or when they are this sick. But it does.

When it is like this, then you know it is love. Have you gotten there yet? Me either. Let's keep working on it.

Today's Response:

With your family, work through the following exercise from 1 Corinthians 13.4–7. Insert your names in the verse instead of the word "love." I would say, "Edwin is patient…" Then make it more specific by adding in your family members' names as objects of love; for example: "Edwin is patient with Tessa…" Discuss among your family if these statements are true and what needs to be done to improve each one.

Point to Ponder:

How well are you following Philippians 2.3–4 in your family? What improvements need to be made?

Today's Prayer:

Loving Father,

Thank You for loving us. We are so unworthy. Help us love others as You have loved us. Help us especially love our families in that way.

Strengthen us to be patient, kind; not to be jealous, brag, be arrogant or behave unbecomingly. Help us not to seek our own, be provoked or take into account a wrong suffered. Help us to rejoice in truth and not unrighteousness and to bear, believe, hope and endure all things. In short, help us be like You in our families.

We love You Father.

Through Your Son we pray,

Amen

Relationship Goal #2: Service

Tabitha, arise!

Acts 9.36–43 has always surprised me. Stephen was stoned in Acts 8, but he was just buried. In Acts 12, James was executed and that was it for him. However, in Joppa a disciple named Tabitha died and immediately an apostle was sent for. The brethren begged him to raise her from the dead and he did.

What is up with that?

No one begged for the deacon and evangelist. No one even begged for the apostle. But there was an outcry for that one sister. Not only that, the request was granted. What special place did this sister hold?

She was a servant!

Don't misunderstand. I fully recognize both Stephen and James were servants. I just want us to see Tabitha was simply and only that. She did not hold an official role in the congregation (though she might have been a "widow indeed"—cf. 1 Timothy 5.3, 9–10). She was not a bishop, deacon or preacher. She was a Christian who served.

We might not think that her service was all that great. All she did was make clothes for widows. What we can say about Tabitha is she did what she could, when she could, for the ones she could. When she was gone, she left a hole. God granted the congregation's request for her return and allowed Peter to raise her from the dead.

Corresponding with our first relationship goal of love, we must push that love into more concrete action through service. Like Tabitha, we need to do whatever we can, whenever we can, for whomever we can. And we need to start with our family.

A Family Full of Foot Washers

Personally, I think some folks today have missed the point of John 13.1–20. We spend so much time arguing over whether or not we should actually wash one another's feet we miss the real example Jesus set.

Keep in mind the historical context of this foot washing. Foot washing was typically the task of the servant for his master. When the master came home after walking in sandals on the dirt walkways, his feet would be swollen, sore and filthy. One of the first things done for the master when he came through the door was washing his feet. When a guest came into our homes, the highly hospitable thing to do was to get the servants to wash their feet.

What would never happen is for the master to wash the feet of the disciples. That was too low and menial. In John 13, Jesus turned the social structure of His day on its head. In the parallel passage of Luke 22.27, Jesus said, "For who is greater, the one who reclines at the table or the one who serves? Is it not the one who reclines at the table? But I am among you as the one who serves."

Jesus, by every right, should have sat at the table being served. Instead, He knelt before His disciples and washed their filthy feet. He served. He honored them in the way a servant would a master. He was the only one who has ever truly been worthy of honor (Revelation 5.12), but instead of demanding the honor and service Himself, He honored and served His disciples. This was unprecedented. No wonder Peter initially rebelled at the thought saying, "Never shall you wash my feet" (John 13.8). Peter did not recognize Jesus is the God who serves. In fact, Jesus said, "The Son of Man did not come to be served, but to serve..." (Matthew 20.28).

After washing their feet, He turned to His disciples and said,

> *Do you know what I have done to you? You call Me Teacher and Lord; and you are right, for so I am. If I then, the Lord and the Teacher, washed your feet, you also ought to wash one another's feet. For I gave you an example that you also should do as I did to you.*

If the Lord could wash the disciple's feet, then the disciples ought to be able to wash one another's feet. That is, if the Master could serve and honor the servants, then the servants ought to serve and honor each other.

This applies in the family as much or more than any other place. We need to be foot washers in our home. Not that we literally have to wash one another's feet. The fact is, you could wash my feet and it really would not be an act of service. But there are lots of things you can do to serve me. Washing my car, cutting my grass, taking me out for lunch are all examples that come quickly to mind. (Perhaps I should spend more time doing this for you.)

Think of all the possibilities in our homes for service. Regrettably, when we think about serving possibilities in the home, we typically think about all the things everyone else can do for us. Remember, however, we are supposed to be the servants. Yes, husbands, we are supposed to serve our wives, not sit on our throne dictating orders she respectfully follows. Yes parents, we are supposed to serve our children, not sit on the sofa directing them to provide our every whim.

We are supposed to be the servant. How can we serve our spouse? …our kids? …our parents? …our siblings? Can we cut their grass, wash their clothes, do their dishes, fix them a meal, change that diaper for them? If we are not going to wash their feet, perhaps there is a time when a nice foot rub will help (or back and shoulder rub). Depending on our family's make-up, it may be service to just spend time talking with them or playing a game. We might serve them with special gifts now and then. Hugs and kisses are always a great way to serve. In fact, just today I heard a presentation that explained the serving nature of a hug. My friend, Elizabeth Pace, explained that a seven second hug causes the body to release endorphins. Endorphins are our bodies' natural pain reliever. These wonderful little guys can lower our blood pressure, relieve stress, decrease pain and even curb hunger. (Let's face it guys, our wives don't need us to fix their problems, they just need us to hold and hug them. And as much as we hate to admit, we need it too.)

How many of us get home and think about all the ways we can serve our family? Usually, we get home thinking about what a rotten day we have had and try to figure out the multiple ways we can prove our day was the worst one so everyone should serve us. Maybe we did have a rotten day and maybe we already know tomorrow will be worse. Keep this in mind—the night Jesus washed His disciples' feet was the night He was going to be arrested and eventually crucified. He knew He was about to go to the cross for these men and for us. He also knew each one of them would flee and save himself, but Jesus served them anyway. Looking a step further, He knew full well Peter, the one who argued with Him, was about to deny Him three times. Jesus washed Peter's feet anyway. What amazes me the most is Jesus knew Judas was about to betray Him. He washed the heel that was about to be lifted up against Him anyway (cf. John 13.18). That is service.

If Jesus could do that for these 12 rash, sometimes rebellious, fickle, ignorant and blatantly disobedient men, how much more ought we be able to serve our families?

A Ransomed Life

In Matthew 20.28, Jesus not only explained that He came not to be served, but to serve, He further described the ultimate service He would render. He came "to give His life a ransom for many."

"Greater love has no one than this, that one lay down his life for his friends" (John 15.13). Greater love has no one than this, that one lay down his life for his family.

This is the great catch of service. This is what stops us in our tracks all too often. Serving means sacrifice. Every moment we spend pursuing someone else's needs and wants are moments we are not pursuing our own needs and wants. If we spend all our time serving others, when do our needs get met?

That is the vulnerable point in the family relationship. Our needs may not get met. Our family may actually walk all over us if we take this approach of service. After all, Jesus came into the world to serve and He was crucified for it. Aren't we glad He made Himself vulnerable for us?

Remember this—no one was ever condemned to hell for being taken advantage of. However, the servant who quit serving but started demanding service and abusing his fellow servants was cast into outer darkness when the true master finally returned (Luke 12.42–48).

However, I believe we can confidently say in most cases, if one person in a family will actually start to ransom their own lives for their family, then the rest will follow suit. By this, I mean really sacrifice self completely. Service is not a manipulation technique to be tried for a day, a week or month and then dropped if you don't see any results in the others. True sacrifice means keeping it up even when the heel is going to be lifted against us.

We must not deceive ourselves. How could we ever think we would actually give up our lives for our family if we won't even give up our favorite television show for them? How could we ever think we would sacrifice ourselves for our family if we won't sacrifice some time for them? How could we ever think we would die for our family if we won't even hurt for them a little?

We must give our lives a ransom for our family. This day is not ours. It is theirs and we should serve them.

Today's Response:

Find out one thing each member of your family would like you to do on a regular basis to serve them. Schedule it and do it.

Point to Ponder:

Why is Jesus' service to His disciples and to us so amazing? What does that service mean to you? What do you think your service will mean to others?

Today's Prayer:

Merciful Father,

We are amazed and humbled at Your service for us. Thank You for Your Son, whose life was ransomed for us. Thank You for Your Spirit, whose revelation guides us into Your will.

Grant us wisdom and strength to sacrifice ourselves in Your service and in service of our family. Help us gain our strength and resolve from You and not wait for others to serve us before we serve. Help us follow the example of Your Son.

We love You Father.

Through Your Son we pray,

Amen

Buy-In Goal: Enjoy the Journey

A Magic Fish

Allow me to share a story I once heard. A recently married young farmer, taking a well-earned day of rest, was out fishing. He had caught about all he wanted, but cast his line out just one last time. He felt the tug and brought in his biggest catch of the day. As he was about to toss the fish into his bucket (you'll never believe this), it began to speak.

"Please, don't throw me in that pile of fish. I am actually a fairy princess trapped in the body of this fish by an evil sorceress. If you let me live and cast me back into the water, I can give you a wonderful gift. Life can be miserable sometimes, but I can grant you the gift to skip those miserable parts. All you will have to do is wish yourself into the future and immediately you will be taken to a future point of life."

The farmer thought this was amazing. He decided to chance it and tossed the fish back in the water. When the fish resurfaced, she said, "I have given you a tremendous gift. Use it wisely and remember you can only move forward; you can never move back into the past. Your body will age, but your mind will only grow the amount of time you actually experience."

Then she sank beneath the surface and was gone. Two days later, the farmer began plowing his fields. He was hot and miserable and he decided to see if the gift really worked. He wished he could skip to the end of the day, going straight to dinner with his wife. No sooner had he made the wish than he was sitting in his house at the dinner table. It was as if his body had kept on doing the work and living his life but his mind had just skipped the day.

After a few more days of work, he decided he had had enough of this and wished he could skip to the end of the harvest. Immediately he found himself at the end of the harvest, ready to sell his crops at the market. "This is not so bad," he thought. "I wonder why that fish said I had to be so careful."

A couple of years went by in this time-skipping fashion and his wife learned she was pregnant. He was so excited. He couldn't wait for another seven months to go by to see his first child. He wished to skip ahead to the day after the birth. The next instant he heard a baby crying in the other room and his wife asking for help.

After a couple of sleepless nights, he wished he could skip ahead to when the child was sleeping all night and potty trained. After having a few more kids, the man just could not believe how stressful it was to raise children. He finally decided just to skip the whole thing. He wished himself to a time when all the children were out of the house.

Though his mind was only a few years older than when he first received the gift, his body had aged quite a bit. He was tired, his body ached most of the time and he just didn't want to work anymore. He wished to skip ahead to when he was old enough to let his kids take care of him.

Suddenly, there he was with his wife and grown children. He listened to their conversation. They were laughing and sometimes crying. The kids were discussing their childhood memories. The farmer's wife was chiming in. However, whenever they turned to the farmer, he only smiled. He couldn't say anything because he did not remember any of it. He had wished it all away. His body was old and could hardly enjoy his present life, and he could not even take joy in happy memories. He had none.

He left the house and walked purposefully to the lake where he had caught the magic fish, crying all the way. Was the fish still alive? Perhaps someone else had caught the fish and not been so generous? It had been many years, how long could a fish, even a magic one, actually live? Even if it was alive, could he find it? If he could find it, would it do anything? After all, it had warned him.

He walked to the bank and waded in a few feet and began to cry out as loud as he could, "Magic fish! It's me the farmer who set you free so many years ago. I have been very foolish and made a terrible mistake. Please, come help me!" He repeated his plea several times, but nothing happened. Finally, he just plopped down in the water, his face in his hands, sobbing. He had missed his life and there was nothing to be done about it.

A moment later the water broke and the fish appeared.

"Hello, farmer," the fish said. "I have already given you one great gift, why should I grant you another?"

"O fairy princess, you warned me not to use your gift unwisely. But I have. I have been foolish beyond belief. My mind is young, but my body is old. I have no fond memories of my life because I wished them all away. Please, take me back to the day I caught you and let me live my life."

"But I told you, you can only go forward, you can never go back. Sending you back to the day you caught me will end the gift I gave you. You will have to endure every trial, every tribulation, every misery and never be able to miss any of it."

"I don't care. I want to live my life. I want to enjoy every minute of every day. I want to see how my wife and I grow closer together. I want to see my children learn to walk and run and live. I want to experience every accomplishment. The tough times will be worth it if only to experience the joy of the good times. I have made it to the end of my life and I have accomplished so much, but I cannot enjoy any of it because I skipped it all."

The fish disappeared beneath the surface of the water and the man cried out, "NO, COME BACK!" He sat there, consumed in his grief, and bowed his head into his hands once again. But then something odd happened. Suddenly, he was no longer sitting in the water. He was dry and sitting in his old boat. His skin was no longer wrinkled and his body no longer ached. He looked up and the fish resurfaced and said, "This was really my gift to you. The ability to skip the miseries of life is really no gift at all. The ability to enjoy the journey is the greatest I can give you. You have set me free, I thank you." The fish disappeared.

The man eagerly paddled his boat to shore. Tied it to a tree and ran to his house. There he found his young wife. He rushed to her, picked her up and kissed her. She never learned what happened to her husband. But she did learn she had married a man who was able to live with the bad days because he knew how to enjoy the journey.

Life's Journey

Obviously, none of us can actually wish days out of our lives. However, many of us wish our lives away. We spend so much time wishing for the day we graduate, the day we marry, the day our first child is born, the day our children graduate, the day we retire. Many of us spend so much time focusing on getting to the end of the journey, we miss the journey. Like the man in our story, we get to the end of life and cannot even enjoy happy memories because we really don't have any.

Too many of us live lives like my dad used to take trips. Like so many other people I have talked to, my dad had a personal goal of beating land speed records. He had figured out exactly what the shortest distance was. He had determined that normal humans only need a bathroom break as often as the car needs gas. It was all about getting to the end of the journey. Granted, I guess we paid some fleeting attention to the scenery whizzing by, but it was a special day if we actually stopped to witness the picturesque outlook on the side of the road or took a scenic detour (we were always going to someday, but on that trip we were in too much of a hurry).

We have to seize the day. We have to learn to enjoy the journey, otherwise we will reach its end and have nothing enjoyable to remember. I have called this the buy-in goal for a reason. I know how easy it is to think about our family goals and develop a Von Trapp family regimen. Do you remember Baron Von Trapp in *The Sound of Music*? The one who commanded his children as he did his soldiers. The one who had a special whistle call for each child. Baron Von Trapp was miserable, and despite his regimen to instill virtue, discipline and success, no one else was having any fun either. None of his kids could wait to get out of the home.

If we end up like him with an extreme educational and spiritual regimen, most of our family members will want to jump ship as well. By 12 months, our children are going to know the books of the Bible and have a well-rounded store of memory verses. By age five, they will learn to spend an hour every morning in prayer and Bible study. By the time they start school, we will have already drilled them in reading, writing and arithmetic. They will know the states and their capitals, the periodic table of elements and be accomplished on at least one musical instrument. On and on the regimen goes. I fully realize that this kind of regimen may actually work for some families. But for most of us, there is no way we can pull this off and actually enjoy being a part of our family.

No matter what our regimen and goals, we have to make sure our home is a place everyone in the family would actually like to be. We have to learn how to have joy. I am not saying our homes should be places of fun and games with few rules and no discipline. I am simply saying we have to learn how to have joy and pursue our goals enjoyably. We must not get so caught up in the pursuit of our lofty goals that every day is spent in misery trying to attain the unreachable.

This Is a Bible Lesson

I know what you are thinking. "Ok, Edwin. That is a great point and you have told some neat stories. But I thought this was a book about what the Bible says about the family." You may be surprised to find that learning to enjoy the journey is a Bible principle.

Read Ecclesiastes 11.7–12.8. This is important. I will include the whole reference here:

> *The light is pleasant, and it is good for the eyes to see the sun. Indeed, if a man should live many years, let him rejoice in them all, and let him remember the days of darkness, for they will be many. Everything that is to come will be futility.*
>
> *Rejoice, young man, during your childhood, and let your heart be pleasant during the days of young manhood. And follow the impulses of your heart and the desires of your eyes. Yet know that God will bring you to judgment for all these things. So, remove grief and anger from your heart and put away pain from your body, because childhood and the prime of life are fleeting.*
>
> *Remember also your Creator in the days of your youth, before the evil days come and the years draw near when you will say, "I have no delight in them"; before the sun and the light, the moon and the stars are dark-*

> *ened, and clouds return after the rain; in the day that the watchmen of the house tremble, and mighty men stoop, the grinding ones stand idle because they are few, and those who look through windows grow dim; and the doors on the street are shut as the sound of the grinding mill is low, and one will arise at the sound of the bird, and all the daughters of song will sing softly. Furthermore, men are afraid of a high place and of terrors on the road; the almond tree blossoms, the grasshopper drags himself along, and the caperberry is ineffective. For man goes to his eternal home while mourners go about in the street. Remember Him before the silver cord is broken and the golden bowl is crushed, the pitcher by the well is shattered and the wheel at the cistern is crushed; then the dust will return to the earth as it was, and the spirit will return to God who gave it. "Vanity of vanities," says the Preacher, "all is vanity!"*

Did you see what God said? He said learn to enjoy the journey. There will be a day when you will not be able to enjoy what is going on down here. While these words were written for the individual to follow, it is important in the family. Learn to enjoy the journey.

Childhood is fleeting. Our children will not get to cuddle with us on Saturday mornings for many more years. Maybe we can wait another thirty minutes to get to all our weekend household chores. If we can afford it, we ought to take that vacation with our family. If we can't afford it, we ought to take one we can. I haven't gotten there yet, but I have heard from many who are older and wiser than me that nobody on their death bed regretted not spending more time in the office. We must not spend so much time wishing away the sleepless nights that we miss the laughter, the hugs and the milestones. Children only take their first step, say their first word and lose their first tooth once. We must not miss these things, but enjoy them to the fullest.

The prime of life is also fleeting. We should follow the desires of our heart while we are able. The goals of success and even the goal of heaven does not mean we are to cloister ourselves in our home as a monastery and never do anything. God actually expects us to enjoy this life, while always remembering and serving Him. Ecclesiastes 8.15 says, "So I commended pleasure, for there is nothing good for a man under the sun except to eat and to drink and to be merry, and this will stand by him in his toils throughout the days of his life which God has given him under the sun." Ecclesiastes 9.7–9 says:

> *Go then, eat your bread in happiness and drink your wine with a cheerful heart; for God has already approved your works. Let your clothes be white all the time, and let not oil be lacking on your head. Enjoy life with the woman whom you love all the days of your fleeting life which He has given to you under the sun; for this is your reward in life and in your toil in which you have labored under the sun.*

Are there going to be dark days too? Of course there are. There will be miseries. There will be trials. There will even be tragedies. We will have fights with our spouses. Our kids will disobey sometimes. Our parents will provoke us every now and again. We will get sick. We will lose jobs. We will even lose loved ones. These, however, are all part of life.

We have to learn, as a family, to look to the silver lining (am I allowed one overused cliché?) We have to learn to rely on each other through the bad times. Amazingly, when the journey is concluding, even those bad times will produce fond memories of family togetherness. We will reach the goal and the journey will have been worth it.

Seize the Day!

Ephesians 5.15–16 says, "Therefore be careful how you walk, not as unwise men but as wise, making the most of your time, because the days are evil."

As Ecclesiastes repeatedly teaches, we have no idea when it is all going to end. Do not get so caught up in getting to the end that you forget to enjoy today. Do not get so caught up in getting your family to the end that you do not enjoy one another today.

Seize this day. Redeem your time this day. Enjoy your wife, your husband, your children, your parents, your brothers, your sisters today. They may not be with you tomorrow. Play games with them. Take a walk with them. Work on a project together with them. Allow them to figure out a way to enjoy whatever it is you are doing. Learn to let them make mistakes and learn from them. Then laugh at the mistakes as you all grow. I am not saying be irresponsible. I am not saying quit working on the goals. I am simply saying make sure you enjoy your journey to the goals.

If you learn how to do this, while remembering your Creator, I can almost guarantee you that your family will enjoy the journey and will be happy to work toward the goal of the journey with you.

I will conclude this chapter with another story I heard as a young man. This comes from the father's perspective, but I imagine you can apply it to your place in the family with little difficulty. It is the story of two sons.

One son stands in the doorway, looking down the street at the approaching car. Hiding behind his mother's legs he carries a look of fear. On the verge of tears, he whispers to his mother, "Daddy is almost home." Another son dashes down the walkway to the roadside. He is grinning as he jumps and shouts back at his mother who rushes out after him. "Mom, Mom, can I wait by the driveway? Daddy is almost home."

I hope I am always that second father. May we always live in such a way that our family can enjoy the journey with us every day. That will help us live through the not so enjoyable days and it will help everyone in our family be happy to continue the journey.

Today's Response:

Plan something fun to do as a family this week. Have a game night, a play-in-the-park afternoon, a picnic or go to a baseball game. Schedule something just to have fun together and make sure to do it.

Point to Ponder:

How much are you enjoying this journey with your family? How much are they enjoying the journey with you? How can you improve this?

Today's Prayer:

Loving God,

Thank You for the numerous blessings You have granted us to enjoy. Thank You for our families. Help us enjoy each other. Help us enjoy our journey together.

Please strengthen us to see the good in each day and to press on through the bad days. Help us live in such a way that as our lives draw to a close we can have precious memories. Thank You for all our happy memories with our family.

We love You Father.

Through Your Son we pray,

Amen

Week Two Group Discussion

- What are the most important lessons you have learned this week?

- What questions do you have about what you learned this week?

- What practical improvement have you and your family made in your family lives based on what you learned this week?

- What practical advice would you give others to accomplish what you learned about this week?

- With what issues do you and your family need help or prayers based on what you learned this week?

- In what activities or kinds of activities do you think every family should participate every week to accomplish the goals you learned about?

- What advice would you give other families to reach the important spiritual goals we have learned about this week and yet still enjoy the journey?

Week Three:
Family Roles

"Nevertheless, each individual among you also is to love his own wife even as himself, and the wife must see to it that she respects her husband. Children, obey your parents in the Lord, for this is right. Honor your father and mother (which is the first commandment with a promise), so that it may be well with you, and that you may live long on the earth. Fathers, do not provoke your children to anger, but bring them up in the discipline and instruction of the Lord."

Ephesians 5.33–6.4

Husbands: Leading with Love

No Dictators Allowed

Many people think John 3.16 is the most well-known verse in the Bible. I am not sure I agree. I think there is one more well-known—at least among Christian husbands.

Ephesians 5.22–23: "Wives, be subject to your own husbands, as to the Lord. For the husband is the head of the wife, as Christ also is the head of the church, He Himself being the Savior of the body."

Too many Christian husbands like to throw their weight around, using this verse as though God gave them absolute dominion in the home. Husbands, this verse does not mean we are the king, the home is our kingdom and the family are our subjects. Our wives and children are not given to us as vassals and slaves to do our bidding. Further, we are not granted the right to unilateral decisions without consideration of our families' needs and desires.

The verse that governs this entire section of scripture is often overlooked. Many people miss that Ephesians 5.22–6.9 is actually an expansion of Ephesians 5.21.

> *"Be subject to one another in the fear of Christ."*

As Paul concluded his section on putting off the old man and putting on the new, he ended with the above statement. One of the differences between the old man and the new is that the old man is self-centered. The new man (or woman), however, submits to others. This is an abbreviated way of teaching what Paul wrote in Philippians 2.3–4: "Do nothing from selfishness or empty conceit, but with humility of mind regard one another as more important than yourselves; do not merely look out for your own personal interests, but also for the interests of others."

Men, we are the heads of our homes, the leaders. However, our headship is not meted out by forcing the family to accomplish our greatest desires. Rather, it means we lead the family to accomplish theirs and, more importantly, God's. Just as Jesus told the apostles, "The kings of the Gentiles lord it over them...But it is not this way with you, but the one who is the greatest among you must become like the youngest, and the leader like the servant" (Luke 22.25–26).

Husbands, the next time you resort to "I am the husband! I am the head! You have to do what I say!" to win an argument or discussion, you need to know you are not following God's plan for leadership.

Having said all of that, we do recognize God has given the husband great responsibility in his role in the home. He *is* the head of the home. This responsibility is mutually exclusive of what the wife or children do. It does not matter how our wives or children behave, whether they fulfill their roles or not, we husbands are to fulfill ours. We are not to be like children, forsaking our responsibilities and then whining that our wives or kids started it.

As we examine Ephesians 5.22–33, we learn two words sum up the role of the husband: Leadership and Love.

Leading Like Christ

Ephesians 5.23 says, "The husband is head of the wife, as Christ also is head of the church." Whether we like it or not, every institution needs a leader. For the church universal and for each local congregation, that person is Jesus Christ. For the family, that person is the husband. To fulfill our responsibilities of leadership in the home, we need to mirror Jesus' leadership of His church.

There are four keys to Christ's leadership of the church we need to mirror in the home.

First, as Christ has authority in the church, so does the husband have authority in the home. According to Ephesians 1.22–23, all things in the church have been placed under Christ's feet. Christ's word is final. We are to follow His lead even if we do not fully understand it. Proverbs 3.5 says, "Trust in the Lord with all your heart and do not lean on your own understanding." So it is with the husband in the home. He is the head. His decisions stand as final and the family is to follow.

However, husbands, remember Christ's headship was qualified in I Corinthians 15.27: "For He has put all things in subjection under

His feet. But when He says, 'All things are put in subjection,' it is evident that He is excepted who put all things in subjection to Him."

The Father, who placed all things in subjection to the Son, is not Himself in subjection to the Son. Rather, He still maintains authority over the Son. In fact, Jesus claimed He did nothing from His own authority, but was submissive to His head, the Father.

"Truly, truly, I say to you, the Son can do nothing of Himself, unless it is something He sees the Father doing..." (John 5.19).

"I can do nothing on My own initiative. As I hear, I judge; and My judgment is just, because I do not seek My own will, but the will of Him who sent Me" (John 5.30).

"For I did not speak on My own initiative, but the Father Himself who sent Me has given Me a commandment as to what to say and what to speak" (John 12.49).

1 Corinthians 11.3 says, "But I want you to understand that Christ is the head of every man, and the man is the head of a woman, and God is the head of Christ." Just as the Son did not lead on His own initiative, but submitted to the Father, husbands are not allowed to lead on our own initiative. Rather, we are to submit to the Son and in turn to the Father. We need to be able to mirror Jesus' statements quoted above from John.

Second, as Christ is the savior of the church, we husbands are to be saviors in our family. Ephesians 5.23 didn't just mention Christ's headship, but also the fact that He is the savior of the body. According to Luke 19.10, "The Son of Man has come to seek and to save that which was lost." Christ exercises His authority for our benefit, not His.

Obviously, we husbands do not provide the sacrifice for salvation. However, husbands, we are to act as the savior of our family. By that I mean we are to sacrifice ourselves and our personal desires in order to provide eternal benefit for our families. We need to realize that being a leader means taking others somewhere. The place we are to be taking our family is heaven.

Hebrews 13.17 has specific reference to leaders in the local congregation, but the passage can also apply to husbands as leaders in the home. "... they keep watch over your souls as those who will give an account." Men, we will give account for how our family fares in judgment. Therefore, we must keep a watch out for their souls.

Do not misunderstand. Obviously, the members of our family will give account for themselves and will not be able to excuse their behavior because of ours. However, when we stand before God in judgment, we must be able to say our wife and children submitted to God because of us and not in spite of us. If they did not submit to God, we had better be able to say it was in spite of us and not because of us.

The long and short of it is this. Husbands do a lot to make sure their wives live in nice houses, wear designer clothes and drive fancy cars. Fathers do a lot to make sure their children get into great extracurriculars, awesome sports programs and good universities. What are we doing to make sure our wife and children get into heaven?

Third, as Jesus sets the example for His church, husbands must be an example for their families. The whole tenor of Ephesians 5.22–33 demonstrates Jesus as our great example. He is the one to whom we can look to know how to lead and how to live. As Peter explained in 1 Peter 2.21, Jesus left us an example to follow in His footsteps. According to Hebrews 2.14–18, Christ was unwilling to simply tell us how to live, but also endured this life that He might be a faithful and merciful High Priest for us. He was unwilling to simply sit on high and issue behavioral edicts. He certainly has never been willing to say, "Do as I say, not as I do."

In like manner, husbands, we need to be examples for our families. Being a leader does not mean standing behind people with a prod and pushing them ahead of us. It means getting out in front and blazing a trail. We must not take our place on high, issuing decisive directions. Rather, we must live properly with and before our families demonstrating faithfulness to God. We must follow advice similar to what Paul told Timothy in 1 Timothy 4.12, "…in speech, conduct, love, faith and purity, show yourself an example of those who believe."

Fourth, as Jesus serves His church, husbands must serve their families. We have already discussed service in this book and even in this chapter. Therefore we won't add much to that here—only to reiterate that Jesus exercises His headship to serve us. He served us by coming into this world. He served us by giving His life as a ransom for many (Matthew 20.28).

> *Have this attitude in yourselves which was also in Christ Jesus, who, although He existed in the form of God, did not regard equality with God a thing to be grasped, but emptied Himself, taking the form of a bond-servant, and being made in the likeness of men. Being found in appearance as a man, he humbled Himself by becoming obedient to the point of death, even death on a cross (Philippians 2.5–8).*

We are to be servants in the home. Our wives and children are not our property or our servants. We are their servants. If you have ever seen the movie *The Princess Bride,* you might remember the only thing the stable boy ever said to Buttercup—"As you wish." Men, perhaps we should learn this phrase. Ask your wife and children what you can do to serve them today?

Love Like Christ

Ephesians 5.25 says, "Husbands, love your wives, just as Christ also loved the church and gave Himself up for her." Husbands are the leaders in the home, but their leadership is governed by love. There are four keys to the love husbands should demonstrate in the home.

First, our love must be unconditional. The term used to describe Christ's love for His church is "agapao." This is the unconditional love we hear so much about. Jesus demonstrated the unconditional nature of His love when He died for us while we were still sinners (Romans 5.6–11; 1 John 4.9–10). Jesus' love for us was not a spontaneous emotional reaction to our lovableness. Rather, it was the conscious choice to do what was best for the unlovable.

In the same way, husbands, we are to love our wives unconditionally, even if she has become our enemy. The love we are commanded is not the spontaneous reaction to our wives' beauty, personality, service or love. It is the conscious choice to do what is best for our wives no matter what. Go back to what we learned in chapter 8 on love. 1 Corinthians 13.4–7 describes how we should love our wives. Further, Colossians 3.19 demonstrates loving our wives properly means refraining from bitterness, resentment and exasperation. Too many believe if love has gone out of their marriages they are allowed to divorce. Husbands, not only is abandoning our marriages not allowed in this situation, neither is the lack of love. Loving our wives is not God's hope, His advice or His goal for our marriages; it is His command.

Second, our love must be sacrificial. In Ephesians 5.25, Jesus demonstrated His unconditional love for His bride by giving Himself up for her. In John 15.13, Jesus said, "Greater love has no one than this, that one lay down his life for his friends."

Husbands, we cannot claim we love our wives if we are not willing to sacrifice ourselves for them. This concept is not just about physically dying for our wives, but about giving up our desires and wants to provide and promote hers. What are we willing to sacrifice for our wives? Are we willing to sacrifice our desire to fix everything to just hold her and listen to her sorrows? Are we willing to sacrifice Monday night football to spend time with her or finish some household project she wants done? Are we willing to sacrifice that higher paying job in order to let her stay closer to her family? Are we willing to sacrifice our day off in order to let her have a day off? Are we willing to sacrifice our "housework and child-raising are for women" mentality in order to do the dishes, laundry, vacuum or change diapers for her? Every marriage and every wife are different. Are you willing to sacrifice whatever it takes to nourish and cherish yours?

Third, we must love our wives by providing for them. Ephesians 4.15–16 says, "…we are to grow up in all aspects into Him who is the head, even Christ…causes the growth of the body for the building up of itself in love." Through His love, Christ provides what the church needs in order to grow. Christ nourishes and strengthens His church.

We husbands are to do the same for our wives. Ephesians 5.28–29 says, "So husbands ought also to love their own wives as their own bodies. He who loves his own wife loves himself; for no one ever hated his own flesh, but nourishes and cherishes it, just as Christ also does the church." Just as we love our own bodies, nourishing and cherishing them, we are to nourish and cherish our wives.

We must nourish our wives, providing not only physical nourishment but also spiritual. Further we are to cherish our wives, providing the emotional support they need. As 1 Peter 3.7 says, "You husbands in the same way, live with your wives in an understanding way..." We are not allowed to toss out the clichéd, "Women, you just can't understand them." We are responsible to learn what makes our wives tick and provide for their needs.

Fourth, we must love our wives by honoring them. Ephesians 5.26–27 says, "...that He might sanctify her, having cleansed her by the washing of water with the word, that he might present to Himself the church in all her glory, having no spot or wrinkle or any such thing; but that she would be holy and blameless." Jesus loved the church, giving Himself up for her that she might be presented to Him in glory. He wanted to glorify us and make us glorious. This encapsulates the idea of honor. Even when we were in our sins, Jesus wanted to honor us. He viewed us as so important He was willing to die for us to help us be the glorious church He knew we could be by His grace.

In the same way, men, we are to honor our wives. We are to present her as glorious, without spot or wrinkle. Peter described this in 1 Peter 3.7 saying, "You husbands...show her honor as a fellow heir of the grace of life, so that your prayers will not be hindered."

We are to honor our wives as fellow heirs of the grace of life. Our wives were so important to Jesus, He died for them. If they were that important to Him, how important ought they be to us? Additionally, Peter said to honor her as someone weaker. That sounds odd until we look up the verse in different translations that speak of our wives as "a weaker vessel." While it may be true that women, in general, have less physical strength than men, I do not believe that is Peter's point. Peter is not saying women are weak and need us men to do everything for them. Rather, the "weaker vessel" is a word picture of precious pottery that is easily broken. We are to envision our wives as a valuable crystal or fine china to be treated with special care. Or we might picture that precious china doll handed down in our family from our great-great grandmother preserved in the curio cabinet to be protected from harm. Our wives are not unbreakable rag dolls to be used, abused and tossed about recklessly. They are not the regular dishware that gets chipped in the dishwasher without our concern because "it is just the everyday stuff." Our wives are precious gems, for which we care and which we protect lest they be broken by us or others. The Proverbialist said, "He who finds a wife finds a good thing and obtains favor from the Lord" (Proverbs 18.22). We must honor her as such.

Remember husbands, we are the leaders in our homes. That does not provide us with great rights; it provides us with great responsibilities. Let us lead our wives and our homes with great love, lest our prayers be hindered, as Peter said in 1 Peter 3.7 and our families be lost. Let us glorify God in our family and lead them to heaven.

Today's Response:

Husbands, ask your wives (and your children) what you can do this week to serve and help them. Schedule it and do it.

Point to Ponder:

Whose goals and desires take precedence in your home? Husband, how can you make it your goal to meet your wife's short and long-term goals and desires?

Today's Prayer:

Merciful Father,

We thank You for Your Son, Jesus, and the example He has established for us. We are amazed at His love, mercy and sacrifice.

We pray especially for our family and the husband in our family. Help him lead in love, submitting to Jesus and in turn to You.

Help us make His job easier as he leads us to heaven and guides us as one who must give account. Forgive us all for when we have failed You in our family.

We love You Father.

Through Your Son we pray,

Amen

Week 3

12

Wives: Helping with Respect

Building Up the Home

Imagine you looked out your window and saw a neighbor lady standing outside her house with a sledge hammer. While her family was still inside, she began hammering away at the house, busting windows, breaking bricks, splintering wood and bringing the home down around her and her family. What would you think?

Now read Proverbs 14.1. "The wise woman builds her house, but the foolish tears it down with her own hands." Regrettably, many women, basing their role on modern cultural ideals instead of on God's Word, have begun to tear down their home with their own hands. Do not get me wrong. I am not saying some concepts of the home and men's leadership have not needed to be corrected. However, some of the modern feminist extremists have thrown the baby out with the bath water. Where issues need to be corrected, then let us do so scripturally. However, we must remember our homes need to be built by the Lord not by modern culture.

Scripturally, the wife's role can be described well with two words—*Help* and *Respect.*

A Suitable Helper

Perhaps the passage that most defines and governs the wife's role in the home is Genesis 2.18: "Then the Lord God said, 'It is not good for the man to be alone; I will make him a helper suitable for him.'" The first wife was created to be a helper to the first husband. In scripture, we find four ways in which wives help their husbands.

First, wives help by doing good to their husbands always. Proverbs 31.10–12 says, "An excellent wife, who can find? For her worth is far above jewels. The heart of her husband trusts in her and he will have no lack of gain. She does him good and not evil all the days of her life."

An excellent wife does not hinder or harm her husband. Rather her help is so great her husband is known in the gates (Proverbs 31.23). That is, he is recognized by the community as a leader and role model. Titus 2.4–5 says older women are to teach the younger women to be kind, loving their husbands. The word for "love" in this passage is a form of the word "philos," which means "friend." Wives are to befriend their husbands.

Regrettably, women are not taught this by modern feminist extremists. To many women in our society, the wife is not the husband's helper. She is his competitor. Her theme song is, "Anything you can do, I can do better." The excellent wife however sings a different tune. She says, "Anything you can do, I can help you do better." Modern feminists do not want women to help their husbands be "known in the gates." They want wives to usurp that position, showing they should have that honor and praise. However, while the excellent wife does not compete for honor in the gates, she receives it anyway. Proverbs 31.31 says, "Give her the product of her hands, and let her works praise her in the gates." The excellent wife receives praise and recognition by helping, not by competing. Where the modern feminist fails, the excellent wife excels.

Second, wives must help their husbands get to heaven. 1 Peter 3.1–2 says, "In the same way, you wives, be submissive to your own husbands so that even if any of them are disobedient to the word, they may be won without a word by the behavior of their wives, as they observe your chaste and respectful behavior."

While we learned in the last chapter that husbands are to take the lead in getting the family to heaven, husbands need their wives' help to get that job done. This is one of the governing motivators for the way they act. As Peter said in 1 Peter 3.7, the wife and husband are fellow heirs of grace. They help each other as any Christian should help a brother or sister get to heaven.

As the wife helps her husband get to heaven, she must remember Galatians 6.1. "Brethren, even if anyone is caught in any trespass, you who are spiritual, restore such a one in a spirit of gentleness; each one looking to yourself, so that you too will not be tempted." Wife, your role of respect does not mean you must sit silently on the sidelines while your husbands sin. Rather you role of helper means you must work to restore him. Keep in mind, however, Paul and Peter agree your help is to be given in gentleness, with a quiet and meek spirit. Your role as helper on the journey to heaven is not to be administered by berating and blistering your husband, even when he has done wrong. Rather, by gently reminding your husband of scripture and by meekly exemplifying the scripture you will help your husband (and your children).

Third, wives help by managing the home. 1 Timothy 5.14 says, "Therefore, I want younger widows to get married, bear children, *keep house*, and give the enemy no occasion for reproach." The term translated "keep house" is the Greek word "oikodespoteo." That word literally means "house ruler." The term does not signify dusting and vacuuming, it signifies managing and running.

This issue is not about who makes the money in the home (read Proverbs 31 again to see how much money a wife can make for the home). Despite who makes the money in the home, wives are to make sure the affairs of the home run smoothly. Wives, you are to make sure the funds are managed so there is food on the table and clothes on the family's backs. You are to make sure the home is a place where all of the family, including yourself, want to be.

Consider Proverbs 31.21, "She is not afraid of the snow for her household, for all her household are clothed with scarlet." Remember when and where this book was written. Snow did not fall very often in Jerusalem. The excellent wife prepared for the future. She considered possible emergencies. Because she was ready, the emergencies were not much of a problem.

Fourth, wives help by guarding the home. Titus 2.5 says wives are to be "sensible, pure, *workers at home*..." The phrase "worker at home" translates the Greek "oikouros," a compound word made up of "oikos," meaning "house," and "ouros," meaning "guard." The word literally means "house guard."

Remember the wise wife builds up the home. One way is as guardian. This does not mean wives make sure the doors are locked and the alarm set. This refers to spiritual guardianship. Wives, you are to stand watch against the evils that would tear down your home from the inside out. You are to guard against the evil influences that would destroy the purity of your husband and children.

Husbands, note very carefully that God has given this role to your wives. I believe God explicitly gave this role to the women because women are typically more sensitive to what is inappropriate than we are. We must allow our wives to establish the standards of decency in our homes (so long as it fits within God's word). Those times when we husbands think she may be going overboard or being too extreme, we need to back off and realize she probably has a better grasp of the situation than we do.

R-E-S-P-E-C-T

Ephesians 5.33 says, "…the wife must see to it that she respects her husband." Aretha Franklin cried out for women's need to receive respect. Certainly, that is true. However, generally speaking, wives feel the need for love, husbands feel the need for respect. Wife, how would you feel if your husband said, "I respect you. I think you are great. You make a great mother. You are great in your job. I just don't love you anymore."? That is exactly how your husband feels when you claim to love him, but do not show him respect. Respect is like oxygen that allows him to breathe. There are three keys to this respect.

First, wives, you are to be subject to your own husbands (Ephesians 5.22). The term for "subject" or "submit" was primarily a Greek military term, which referred to arranging troops under the command of a leader. In non-military use, it was voluntarily giving in, cooperating, assuming responsibility and carrying a burden. This term says absolutely nothing about the relative importance of the one submitting to the one in authority. This is simply a term of roles on a team. We need to understand God's system of having one in authority and others who submit is a practical issue. Any group working together to accomplish goals must have a leader who has final authority where the buck stops. Others must follow. It is that way in the church, in the business world, in sports teams and in our families.

You are to submit to your own husband. You are not to submit to your friends' or co-workers' ideas of how your family should be. You are not to submit to popular opinion. You are certainly not to submit to someone else's husband. You are to submit to your own husband. The only exception to this is found in the principle of Acts 5.29. "We must obey God rather than men." You must not submit to any direction that contradicts the will of God.

Second, wives, you are to submit to your husbands as to the Lord. Paul is quite clear and leaves no room for equivocation on this point in Ephesians 5.22. Not only are you to submit to your husbands, you are to do so as to the Lord. Ephesians 5.24 goes on to say, "But as the church is subject to Christ, so also the wives ought to be to their husbands in everything." In other words, how would you respond if God almighty were the one making the decision? That is the way you are to treat your husbands final decisions.

Of course, someone will say, "If God almighty were standing here, He would not be acting the way my husband is acting." Regrettably, that is true too often. However, remember what Peter said in 1 Peter 3.1–2. Even if your husband is not obeying the word, whether a Christian or otherwise, your responsibility is to submit respectfully. Amazingly, Peter points out that in this way, husbands will be won. That is, through a wife's submission many ungodly husbands will be turned to godliness. Regrettably, most wives today do not take this approach. Rather, when their husbands live in an ungodly fashion and treat them abominably, they rise up and rebel, laying down ultimatums and threats. While we all fully understand this response, we have to recognize it is neither biblical nor helpful. Though I cannot guarantee it works all of the time, I have seen and heard of the submission of wives working wonders in husbands' lives. I have never yet seen or heard of the rebellion of a wife who has finally had enough bring a husband to repentance.

Third, wives, you are to respect your husbands unconditionally. Ephesians 5.33 says, "Nevertheless, each individual among you also is to love his own wife even as himself, and the wife must see to it that she respects her husband." Just as we husbands learned in the last chapter to love you unconditionally, God gives no caveats to remove you responsibility to respect your husband.

Far too many wives decide they will obey their husbands, but they spend their whole time arguing with him about it. Then, if the husband's decision does in fact turn out to be incorrect, which it sometimes will, they take the opportunity to say, "See, I told you so." This is not respect.

Just as we husbands are to honor you, our wives, the Lord has said you must treat us with respect. We noted above that the love younger women are to be taught to have for their husbands in Titus 2.5 was from the Greek word "phileo." That kind of love carries the idea of a relational love that says, "I esteem and adore you above all others."

However, I have known many unrespectable husbands. Their wives consistently ask, "How can I respect this man?" The answer is to find something, anything, even if it is a small thing, and start demonstrating your respect for him in that area. At the same time, stop verbally and visibly disrespecting him for the things he does that are not so pleasing. You will be amazed at the impact that will have on your husband.

Wives, as we conclude this look at your role to help your husband with respect, remember what we learned about the husband's role. It applies to you as well. Your role as wife is mutually exclusive of your husband's and children's behavior. No matter how they behave, this is your role and your responsibility. Gain your strength from God and be the respectful helper God created you to be. When you do, your name will be praised in the gates. Your children will rise up and call you blessed and your husband will say of you, "Many daughters have done nobly, but you excel them all" (Proverbs 31.29).

Today's Response:

Wife, ask your husband what you can do this week to help him. Schedule it and do it.

Point to Ponder:

Do you spend more time competing with your husband or complementing your husband? If you asked your husband, what would he say? How can you improve your respect and help?

Today's Prayer:

Heavenly Father,

You are worthy of glory and honor. We submit to You because You are holy, righteous and awesome.

We pray for Your strength in our family. Please be with the wife in our family that she will have the commitment to help with respect, loving her husband and her family.

Bless our marriage that we may grow closer to one another as we draw closer to You. Be glorified by our relationship.

We love You Father.

Through Your Son we pray,

Amen

Parents: Bring Them Up

A Blessing from God

> *Behold, children are a gift of the Lord,*
> *The fruit of the womb is a reward.*
> *Like arrows in the hand of a warrior,*
> *So are the children of one's youth.*
> *How blessed is the man whose quiver is full of them;*
> *They will not be ashamed*
> *When they speak with their enemies in the gate.*
> Psalm 127.3–5

I recognize these words were penned in a more agrarian society. I know in a farming community, kids were a great blessing because they were free labor. However, I do not think this passage ceased to be true in the Industrial Revolution. Children are a blessing.

As with any gift from the Lord, we must be good stewards. God has not given us children to do with as we choose. We are to raise them in a way that glorifies Him. Based on our culture, we get about 18 years to train them up and then we hand them back to God, sending them out in the world to be His tools.

We have to ask, how are we doing with this stewardship? How can we be trustworthy in this stewardship? There are several passages we will note. Some specifically address fathers, some mothers. However, we know the parents are to help each other. We recognize each passage applies to the parents in general, working together as a team to raise godly offspring.

Bring Them Up

Ephesians 6.4 says, "Fathers, do not provoke your children to anger, but bring them up in the discipline and instruction of the Lord."

A regrettable fact of modern parenthood is few parents have ever sat down and determined what their goal as parents is. Our goal is not simply to make it through today. Our goal is not to provide our children with pleasures, entertainments or enjoyments. Our goal is not to give them everything we did not have as children.

Our goal is to "bring them up." The word translated here, "*ektrepho*," means "to nourish up to maturity." Our general approach to raising children, the way we interact, the experiences we provide, the way we discipline needs to push them toward maturity.

A second regrettable fact of modern parenthood is most parents do not measure their success based on the progressive maturity of their children. Usually, parents base their assessment of success on whether or not their children are having a good time. Therefore, we have a generation of young adults who do not behave responsibly. Rather, they act based on feelings and pleasures.

I am not saying you should raise your children to be miserable. Rather, I believe we find one of the great paradoxes of child-raising. True happiness does not come by doing what gives us pleasure at the moment. True happiness comes as a result of doing what is right, responsible and mature—actions that are not always pleasurable in the moment. Hebrews 12.11 exemplifies this paradox: "All discipline for the moment seems not to be joyful, but sorrowful; yet to those who have been trained by it, afterwards it yields the peaceful fruit of righteousness."

No doubt, we must raise our children to physical maturity. However, physical maturity is the smallest aspect of our goal. After all, in most cases, as long as we keep feeding our kids, they will make it to physical maturity. This maturity is "in the Lord." Our goal is to bring our children up to mental, emotional and spiritual maturity. Too often parents provide an entertaining and pleasurable childhood. Their top goals for raising their kids are to get them a car and put them through college. They send their kids to school to produce mental maturity; experience will give them emotional maturity; and spiritual maturity… "Well, that's why we go to church." Thus, we have a great outcry in modern religion for youth ministers and youth groups. Parents, these responsibilities do not belong to the government or the church—they belong to us. Perhaps the government and the church can help us, but they will not be the ones who stand before God and give account for how our children were raised.

Do Not Provoke

Ephesians 6.4 began by saying we are not to provoke our children to anger. Colossians 3.21 says, "Fathers, do not exasperate your children, so that they will not lose heart." Paul gives this command, I believe, because it is too easy for us to get so caught up in our own lives that we neglect our children and their emotional needs, provoking them or exasperating them.

I think of a great example of this in the Disney movie, *The Kid*. In the beginning of the movie, we see the dreadful relationship nearly 40 year old Russ Duritz has with his father. His father needed help moving. Wealthy Russ sent him a check to pay for a mover because his time was worth more than a mover's. His father suggested he might want some of his childhood belongings. Russ asked how many times he had ever asked his dad for anything. Russ had clearly lost heart in his relationship with his dad.

Later, due to unexplained movie magic, Russ is reminded of his early childhood relationship with his father by his time traveling younger self. Eight year old Rusty explains how much he liked to help his dad. But sometimes he made mistakes and his dad yelled at him. He told about a time when he had recently helped his dad but lost a screw. He found it later and was waiting to give it to his dad.

Eventually, we see the point at which little Rusty lost heart, becoming the dispirited and exasperated Russ Duritz. Rusty did not know his mother was dying. Some bullies had picked a fight with him at school and his mother had to come pick him up. As they arrived at home, his father pulled into the driveway understandably upset that his very sick wife had wearied herself by leaving the house. He came out to the walkway where he had commanded little Rusty to wait. While we can perhaps understand the father's reaction, we still see that he was caught up in his own issues and not paying attention to his son's needs. As he chewed Rusty out for making his mother leave the house he said, "What is the matter with you? How could you do this to your mother? What are you trying to do, kill her faster? We're gonna lose her and you pull a stunt like you did today. You're killing her." Rusty, not able to process what he just learned, began crying and reverted back to what made sense to him. He pulled out the screw as though giving it back would fix the problem and said, "I found the screw, Dad. Here it is. Look at it." His father's response was, "Stop crying. Stop crying. Stop. You got to grow up now, do you understand? Grow up. Grow up!" and he walked off.

In this movie, 40 year old Russ was able to witness this as an adult and understand what happened. His father had reacted not so much out of anger and meanness, but out of fear. He was losing his wife and did not know how to deal with it. Therefore, Russ was able to forgive his dad and fix their relationship. But here is the reality: Parents—our little children are not going to travel into the future and explain to their adult counterparts what happened to them as kids. The wounds we inflict on our children because we are so caught up in our own issues that we don't help them will provoke them, exasperate them and cause them to lose heart. We must not let that happen.

Do not misunderstand. This passage does not say if our children ever get angry with us, we have failed. Sometimes, when we do our jobs properly they will get angry. They may even lash out with painful words such as, "I hate you!" and "I never want to see you again!" In these cases, if we have been treating them properly, our children are becoming angry without real provocation.

In opposition to provocation, Paul taught parents to love their children and be kind in Titus 2.4–5. The word for love in this verse is from the Greek word "phileo," which, as we have already learned, refers to the relational love of friends. Parents, we must learn to be friends with our children, being kind to them, looking out for their physical, emotional, mental and spiritual needs.

We might ask how parents can provoke their children to wrath. They do so in much the same way anyone is provoked to wrath or exasperated. Allow me to share a list of 20 actions that will provoke your children. It is not exhaustive, but gives a good idea of the kind of actions that will negatively impact our children. Some of these actions will immediately provoke our children. Others will do so when they become adults and learn what we have done to them. When I originally compiled this list, it was in the context of fathers provoking their children. I am going to leave it in that form. I have no doubt, mothers, you will be able to apply the list to yourself as well.

1. Lie to them (after all, they are too young to know the difference).
2. Break your promises and commitments (they will never remember).
3. Never admit when you are wrong and certainly don't apologize (they are just kids, a big man like you doesn't have to answer to them).
4. Always expect too much of them (they ought to be able to do what you can do).
5. Always expect too little of them (they are only little kids and challenging them to grow, improve or mature might be too much for their delicate self-esteem).
6. Do not clearly explain your expectations and then punish them severely when they fall short (they are your children, they ought to know exactly what you meant whether you told them or not).
7. The only expectation you should make clear is that you expect them to mess everything up, making sure to remind them of this before they ever try anything new (they are kids and they have messed up in the past, why should this time be any different?).
8. When they do accomplish something properly, do not encourage or praise them, instead, say, "It's about time you got something right" (it is about time, isn't it?).
9. Do not correct them when they do something wrong (kids love growing up, starting a family and *then* finding out the way they act has ruined their lives).

10. Demean them and degrade them by hollering and yelling at them a lot, especially in front of their friends (your kids are surely hard of hearing and must not have heard you the first time).
11. Constantly threaten them with punishments, but never follow through until you are really mad (kids like to know their parents instructions do not mean anything unless they are angry).
12. Vent your frustration, anger and embarrassment on them when you punish them (if you are not frustrated, angry or embarrassed, there is no reason to discipline them anyway, is there?).
13. Be inconsistent with them, especially in discipline (kids like to get away with things and this gives them the perfect chance to try).
14. Never let them know where they stand with you (kids like guessing games).
15. Constantly remind them how immature, childlike, ignorant, stupid and worthless they are. Do this while you are yelling and hollering at them in front of their friends (kids are amazingly resilient, will probably forget the bad things you called them and will surely enjoy the challenge of proving you wrong).
16. Do not forgive them when they repent, instead hold grudges, bring up past behavior and generally just act like you are always mad at them (that will make it more meaningful when you tell them you love them in their birthday cards).
17. Never explain how life really works to your children (they will enjoy the challenge of figuring it out on their own when they get to work and learn their boss doesn't care about their self-esteem, expects them to do their job right the first time, clean up

their own messes and actually earn the money he gives them by working for it).

18. Do not spend time with them in meaningful interaction and conversation, instead spend all your time working so you can room them in a nice house, feed them in the nicest restaurants and buy them all the neatest toys and gadgets (they know you want all these things you didn't get to have when you were a kid. I'm sorry, I meant they know you want them to have all the things you didn't get to have when you were young. Besides, when you die, they won't really want to remember anything about you, they will just want to know who gets the house).
19. Do not teach your children how to work or handle the money they earn from it (it makes them feel responsible, mature and successful when they have to ask you to support their kids because they do not know how).
20. Finally, dads, if you want to provoke your children to wrath, treat their mother like dirt (they love to see examples of strength, power and authority and they especially like to see the person who is most dear to them getting abused).

Discipline and Instruction

Paul taught that instead of provoking our children to wrath, we should "bring them up in the discipline and instruction of the Lord" (Ephesians 6.4). The two terms translated here, "*paideia (discipline)*" and "*nouthesia (instruction)*," are somewhat interchangeable. However, they both carry slightly different shades of meaning. The former, "discipline," emphasizes training with action, while the latter, "instruction," emphasizes training with words.

Training with action may include several aspects. Because the term is translated "discipline" we are likely to think first and foremost about training with the rod. As Hebrews 12.5–6 demonstrates, training with the rod is a loving approach to childrearing when used properly. Despite our modern cultural fear of the rod, the Bible clearly teaches the maxim—"Spare the rod and spoil the child" (see Proverbs 13.24; 22.15; 23.13–14; 29.15).

However, please use some common sense guidelines when applying the rod. Use it as a tool to produce maturity, not a tool to vent anger or embarrassment. Use it consistently, not sporadically. Use it with future results in mind, not the present moment. Use it as quickly as possible, not when a lot of yelling and counting has failed. Finally, when you are done using it, make sure you explain to the child why you used it and reaffirm your love to them (do not mistake this for gushing over the child in an effort to win their love back).

Another action-based training is to let the children face the natural consequences of their actions. Read the approach wisdom takes to training each of us in Proverbs 1.24–29. If your children break a window, make them work to pay for it. If they misuse a possession, take it away either temporarily or permanently. Or develop an illustration that will help them envision the consequences of their actions. The story is told of a woman who had passed on a juicy tidbit of information about a friend only to find out it wasn't true. She went to a wise matron in her village to find out how to fix her error. The woman told her to go home and get a feather pillow, rip it open and spread the feathers out on the road back to the wise matron's house. When she got back the wise woman told her to go back and pick up all the feathers. The woman stepped outside and rushed back in saying, "I can't do it, the wind has blown all the feathers away. What will I do?" The wise woman explained, "So it is with gossip. Once you have passed on a story, you can never go back and recollect it." Think of creative ways to demonstrate consequences to your children.

Practicing good behavior is also a means of training through action. Every year sports teams host training camps. What do they do? Sit around and listen to a lot of talk? Do they get chastened with the rod? No, they get trained. They perform drill after drill after drill. When they get to game time, the plays are engrained in their minds and happen naturally. Drill your children. Don't wait until you get in the assembly to discipline them for how they act. Have them practice at other times.

We can probably more readily grasp training through words—Instruction. Straightforward teaching is one way. Deuteronomy 6.7 provides a good structure for that. Teach your children when you sit in the house (how about meal times or just shutting the tv off some nights and talking), when you walk in the way (turn the radio, cd player or dvd machine off and talk as a family while you travel in the car), when you lie down (bedtime) and when you rise up (get up early enough to have time to talk).

Jesus used a great means of verbal instruction. He told stories. Do you remember the Parables of the Sower, the Good Samaritan, the Talents? Tell them stories from your childhood or stories about members of your family. Tell them stories about heroes and role models. Read to them. Then discuss what they learned from the stories.

Obviously, we have to reprove and rebuke our children when they have done wrong. However, as we are restoring our children, we need to do it gently as Galatians 6.1 demonstrates.

Finally, we often make sure to call our kids on the carpet when they do something wrong. We also need to roll out the red carpet when they do things right. Encourage and praise them as often as you can. Remember, they are children. They will not do everything as well as you, so don't withhold praise and encouragement until they get it exactly right. Learn to praise and encourage them when they improve as well.

*****

Raising kids is not always easy. It takes planning, preparation and perseverance. However, through the grace of God, we can do it. We need to make one final point. Kids really are amazingly resilient. We are going to make mistakes. However, if we learn to apologize for them, our children will be amazingly forgiving. They will not "end up on Oprah" just because we didn't do everything 100% right all the time. Don't spend too much time worrying about whether or not you are ruining your kids. Simply follow God's word, admit when you messed up, apologize and do your best again tomorrow. You and your kids will make it.

Today's Response:

Parents, what will you do this week to specifically help lead your children further on the road to maturity.

Point to Ponder:

Envision your children when they are leaving your home. How do you want them to behave? What do you want them to know? What do you want to be important to them? What do you need to do now and in the years to come to bring that goal about?

Today's Prayer:

Heavenly Father,

Thank You so much for our children. They are indeed a blessing and bring us so much joy and happiness.

Help us raise them in Your nurture and admonition, not provoking them to anger but bringing them up in Your discipline and instruction.

Give us patience and help us remember what it was like to be a child. Help us balance accepting them where they are and challenging them to be more in Your service.

Please, forgive our failures.

We love You Father.

Through Your Son we pray,

Amen

Children: Obeying with Honor

Its Tough Being a Kid

Let's face it. It is tough being a kid. Here we are trying to figure out what life is all about. Too often our parents have forgotten what it was like to be a child and they just don't understand what we are going through. We want to contribute, but nobody really wants to listen. We want to know, "Why?" but nobody wants to tell us. We are fighting to be independent, but everything pushes us to dependence.

Perhaps it will help to remember that Jesus, God in the flesh, was also a child once. He went through all the hardships of childhood and adolescence just like we have to. Notice how He lived through childhood according to Luke 2.52: "And Jesus kept increasing in wisdom and stature, and in favor with God and men."

As you consider your role in the family, this verse should always guide you. Do not cop out like most of the kids you go to school with, thinking childhood is about X-Box and X-Men. You are supposed to be growing up. Do not be satisfied with where you are now; you need to increase, not just in stature (height and weight) but also in wisdom. Further, you need to learn to please God and men. You need to learn to be a person God is happy to call His child and learn to be someone other people enjoy being around.

Your role at home as you grow is summarized with three words—*Obedience*, *Honor* and *Joy*.

Children, Obey Your Parents

In Ephesians 6.1, Paul wrote, "Children, obey your parents in the Lord, for this is right." Moses said, "As for the days of our life, they contain seventy years, or if due to strength, eighty years" (Psalm 90.10). If you meet Moses' expectations, you will spend about ¼ of your life living in your parents' home. While you are there, you are charged by God to obey them.

The friends you hang with, the tv shows and movies you watch, the music you listen to will act as though this is really not important. However, to God, it is of utmost importance. In Romans 1.30, God placed disobeying your parents right up there with murder, homosexuality, inventing evil and hating God. God takes this obedience to parents thing very seriously.

In fact, under the Old Covenant, if a child was rebellious and self-willed, refusing to obey his parents or accept their chastisement, the parents could take the child to the elders of the city as a final recourse and have him stoned to death (Deuteronomy 21.18–21).

There is a lot of confusion about what it means to obey parents. Obeying your parents does not mean finally doing what they say when they have yelled and screamed. It does not mean doing what they say by the time they have counted to 2 ½. It does not mean doing what they say because you wanted to do it anyway. It does not mean doing what they say because they are going to give you an allowance for it.

Obeying your parents means doing what they say the first time they say it. It means doing what they say without complaining. It means remembering the responsibilities they have given you on your own. It means doing what they say even if you don't understand why, don't want to or think it is a waste of time.

Part of obedience means accepting discipline. Proverbs 13.1 says, "A wise son accepts his father's discipline, but a scoffer does not listen to rebuke." Likewise, Proverbs 15.5 says, "A fool rejects his father's discipline, but he who regards reproof is sensible."

As shocking as it may seem, being disciplined is for your own good. Hebrews 12.7–11 says:

> *It is for discipline that you endure; God deals with you as with sons; for what son is there whom his father does not discipline? But if you are without discipline, of which all have become partakers, then you are illegitimate children and not sons. Furthermore, we had earthly fathers to discipline us, and we respected them; shall we not much rather be subject to the Father of spirits, and live? For they disciplined us for a short time as seemed best to them, but He disciplines us for our good, so that we may share His holiness. All discipline for the moment seems not to be joyful,*

> *but sorrowful; yet to those who have been trained by it, afterwards it yields the peaceful fruit of righteousness.*

The Hebrew writer relates being disciplined by parents to being disciplined by God. Obviously, in the moment that you are spanked, grounded or otherwise punished, it is no fun. However, in time you will come to respect your parents for the way they have helped you. In time, you will enjoy peaceful fruits from righteousness and wise living because your parents loved you enough to discipline you.

Proverbs 13.24 says, "He who withholds his rod hates his son, but he who loves him disciplines him diligently." Further, just to show how important it is for your parents to chastise and discipline you, read Proverbs 23.13–14: "Do not hold back discipline from the child, although you strike him with the rod, he will not die. You shall strike him with the rod and rescue his soul from Sheol." Sheol is the realm of the dead, the Hebrew equivalent to Hades. Your parents' discipline is actually a gift of life. I am not saying you have to enjoy it. However, you do need to accept it, learn from it and be thankful for it.

Allow me to address one regrettable situation I see happening too often. Perhaps your parents are divorced. Too often, one parent will want to attract you to his/her side by letting you do what you want. The other will still want to help you grow to maturity, striving to maintain a standard of discipline. I know it is hard to see this now, but believe me, if you are in this situation, it will be better for you in the long run to stay with and listen to the one who disciplines you. Don't be deceived, that parent is the one who really loves you.

There is only one qualifier on this command of obedience. Paul said to obey your parents "in the Lord." If your mother or father ever asks you to do something that contradicts what God says in the Bible, then you may disobey your parents. As Peter said in Acts 5.29, "We must obey God rather than men." But that is the only exception.

Honor Your Father and Mother

When Paul said you must "honor your father and mother" in Ephesians 6.2, he pointed out it was the first commandment with promise. He referred back to the 10 commandments under the Old

Covenant. In that list, honoring parents was the first one that mentioned a specific blessing. That blessing was, "That it may be well with you, and that you may live long on the earth." Honoring your parents has an actual impact on your life.

As with obedience, this command is extremely important to God. Under the Old Law, disrespect to parents was punishable by death (Exodus 21.17).

Honoring your parents means always speaking to them with respect and honor. "Yes, sir;" "No, sir;" "Yes, ma'am" and "No, ma'am" ought to be a common part of your conversation with them. "Please," "thank you" and "you're welcome" should always accompany requests, granted petitions and thanks given to you. You should never interrupt your parents when they are speaking (unless there is a major emergency). Any interruption you do have to make should begin with something like "excuse me, please." You should never speak to your parents with a sarcastic, bitter or resentful tone of voice. Never back talk your parents and never try to manipulate them.

Further, and I know this one is going to be the tough one, you should always speak about your parents with great respect. Something funny happens as we grow up. For several years, we spend all our time arguing with other kids about how much better our parents are than theirs. Then a day comes when parents are no longer cool. They become an embarrassment to us. You need to be an exception. You need to always speak about your parents as though they are the greatest people on earth. You should not call them names or speak badly of them behind their backs to your friends. It would also be good if you tried to stand up for your friends' parents every now and then.

Let me share with you a passage that has always shocked me. Proverbs 30.17 says, "The eye that mocks a father and scorns a mother, the ravens of the valley will pick it out, and the young eagles will eat it." Granted, this is a proverb, a maxim, and is not to be taken absolutely literal. However, the point is God despises a disrespectful attitude. Rolling your eyes or looking at your parents as if they are stupid is not allowed by God and will be punished severely.

Part of honoring your parents is respecting their wisdom. We have to come to grips with the fact that our parents have lived in this world longer than we have. They may well have forgotten what it was like to be a child or a teenager, however, they know more about life than we do. We should be like sponges soaking up the wisdom they have to offer. Proverbs 1.8–9 says, "Hear, my son, your father's instruction and do not forsake your mother's teaching; indeed, they are a graceful wreath to your head and ornaments about your neck."

You may be shocked to find out your parents went through just about everything you are going through. I certainly hope that as your parents instruct you, they do so with patience and understanding. But even if they do not, you need to recognize their wisdom, gain their counsel and learn from their instruction.

Further, honoring your parents means learning to make a return to them. Your parents shouldered a great responsibility in raising you. They have fed and clothed you. They have provided you with a bed to sleep in and a house to live in. They have acted as your chauffer driving you to school, practice, club meetings, worship and whatever else you have had going on. Your parents have done these things expecting nothing in return. God, however, expects you to make a return to them.

Paul addressed this in 1 Timothy 5.4, "If any widow has children or grandchildren, they must first learn to practice piety in regard to their own family and to make some return to their parents..." Then in 1 Timothy 5.8, "If anyone does not provide for his own...he has denied the faith and is worse than an unbeliever."

If you are one of the unfortunate few to have had parents who did not take care of you, but abused you, please consider Luke 6.27–28: "But I say to you who hear, love your enemies, do good to those who hate you, bless those who curse you, pray for those who mistreat you." This book is not intended to work you through the issues of an abusive childhood. There are other books designed for that. I do believe by God's grace you can overcome. Let me point out even you need to find some place where you can honor your parents. Hopefully, as you work through that process, your parents will learn their wrongs and repent and you will all be able to work toward healing.

Rejoice During Your Childhood

Perhaps I shocked you above when I pointed out that the third word that summarized your role as a child was Joy, but that is a biblical concept. Ecclesiastes 11.9–10 says:

> *Rejoice, young man, during your childhood, and let your heart be pleasant during the days of young manhood. And follow the impulses of your heart and the desires of your eyes. Yet know that God will bring you to judgment for all these things. So, remove grief and anger from your heart and put away pain from your body, because childhood and the prime of life are fleeting.*

God expects you to enjoy your youth. Do what you enjoy. Follow the desires of your heart. If you want to learn how to play the guitar or the drums, do it. If you want to play soccer, baseball or football, go for it. If you want to travel (and can afford it) go for it. Through all of this, God simply asks that you remember Him. Keep Him first. Whatever you do, you are still to seek first His kingdom and righteousness (Matthew 6.33). However, enjoy your youth; you only get it once.

At the same time, you need to make sure you are a joy to your parents. Proverbs 23.24–25 says, "The father of the righteous will greatly rejoice, and he who sires a wise son will be glad in him. Let your father and your mother be glad, and let her rejoice who gave birth to you." Live in such a way your parents can be proud of you and enjoy you. The principle of Hebrews 13.17 applies here. Let me paraphrase it in a parent-child context. "Obey your parents and submit to them, for they keep watch over your souls as those who will give an account. Let them do this with joy and not with grief, for this would be unprofitable for you." Be a joy to your parents, not a grief.

As Jesus did, you need to keep increasing in wisdom and stature, and in favor with God and men. I know being a kid is not easy. Take it from me, if you don't take the approach to childhood described in this chapter and in the Bible passages we have noted, it will never get any easier. However, if you follow God's advice in your childhood, you will eventually enjoy the peaceful fruit of righteousness.

Today's Response:

Children, ask your parents what will help them enjoy your presence in the home even more. Ask them what you can do to be more helpful this week. Schedule it and do it.

Point to Ponder:

What do you think it means that Jesus increased in stature, wisdom and favor with God and men? What do you think you need to do to follow Jesus' footsteps in this?

Today's Prayer:

Heavenly Father,

Thank You, God, for our parents. They have done so much for us. We pray that You bless them and strengthen them. Help us live in such a way as to bring them joy.

Help us obey and honor our parents, speaking to them and about them with great respect.

Please forgive us for when we have disobeyed them and help us accept and learn from their discipline as we accept and learn from Yours.

We love You Father.

Through Your Son we pray,

Amen

Siblings: Friends and Brothers (or Sisters)

Our Darkest Day

I believe most would concede the darkest days in the history of the United States were the days of the Civil War. During that time men from one nation did not fight men from another. Rather, countrymen stood on the field of battle and fired upon each other. The travesty of this period was amplified by the families divided—brother fought against brother.

Abraham Lincoln borrowed Jesus' words as he addressed the Republican Convention on June 16, 1858 to describe the situation. "A house divided against itself cannot stand" (cf. Matthew 12.25).

No matter their opinion of the war, its causes and consequences, everyone sees this battle of brother against brother as tragic. Yet, how often does a civil war in miniature occur within families today. Brother fights against brother. Sister against sister. Parents take sides and play favorites. Such a state is tragic. In Psalm 35.14, David explained how nobly he treated his enemies when they were sick and afflicted. He wrote, "I went about as though it were my friend or brother." David treated his enemies as brothers. Regrettably, far too many people treat their brothers as enemies.

Every family needs to remember that a house divided against itself cannot stand. You may be surprised to find out that the Bible says a great deal about the relationship between brothers and sisters. In a very real sense, nearly every page of the Bible addresses this issue. As God told the Israelites how to behave toward each other, the motive He impressed upon them was that they were brethren. Then as God revealed the New Covenant and instituted His church, He described the church as a family. The proper treatment of brothers and sisters is considered so naturally understood God used it to describe how we ought to treat other Christians.

1 Timothy 5.1–2 says, "Do not sharply rebuke an older man, but rather appeal to him as a father, to the younger men as brothers, the older women as mothers, and the younger women as sisters, in all purity." 1 Peter 3.8 says, "To sum up, all of you be harmonious, sympathetic, *brotherly*, kindhearted, and humble in spirit." Instead of "brotherly," the New King James Version says, "love as brothers."

This demonstrates just about every statement in the Bible speaking of how the Israelites were to treat each other and how Christians are to treat each other will teach us principles for how brothers and sisters ought to treat each other.

Biblical Examples

The Bible is filled with examples of brothers and sisters and how they treated each other. Regrettably, many of them were dreadful examples. We can learn from them, both the bad and the good.

Sadly, the very first murder in the Bible was committed between brothers. Cain, jealous that God accepted Abel's sacrifice, did not learn from his brother. Rather, he fed upon his jealousy and killed him (Genesis 4.8). Jealousy has no place between brothers and sisters.

Jacob and Esau had a dreadful relationship. In Genesis 25.27–34, while Esau certainly despised his birthright, Jacob took advantage of his brother to gain it. Then in Genesis 27, Jacob, at his mother's instigation, deceived Isaac and stole Esau's blessing. No wonder Esau wanted to kill his brother (Genesis 27.41).

On a positive note, while Jacob and Esau spent 20 years apart, both of them apparently grew. When Jacob returned, he came humbly offering great gifts to the brother of which he once took advantage (Genesis 32.13–21). Further, Esau learned to forgive Jacob such that he initially refused to take Jacob's gift (Genesis 33.9).

Rachel and Leah were sisters. Due to Laban's treachery, Jacob married them both. Regrettably, Jacob treated Rachel with favoritism that developed a competition between the sisters. Genesis 29–30 demonstrates the contest between the two as they actually used their children against each other. Competition, in this sense, has no place among brothers and sisters. Perhaps it was this dreadful competition and envy that motivated God to make it illegal under Moses' law for one man to marry sisters (Leviticus 18.18).

The rivalry between Leah and Rachel surely paved the way for the terrible rivalry between Joseph and his brothers. However, I am certain Joseph's eagerness to tell his dreams of greatness to his brothers did not help (cf. Genesis 37.5–11). Further, Jacob's favoritism of Rachel among his wives led to favoritism of her son, Joseph, above these brothers. All of this led to jealousy and enough hatred that the brothers conspired together at first to kill, but then sell Joseph into slavery (cf. Genesis 37.18–36).

The Bible does not tell us much about Joseph's feelings about his brothers during his years of slavery and imprisonment. But when they turned up to ask for food, we see an interesting story. Joseph first tested them to see if they had changed at all. They had. Once, they had been willing to kill the child who was their father's favorite. Now they were willing to sacrifice themselves and their own children to protect their father's new favorite, Benjamin (Genesis 42–45). Additionally, even when Joseph's father died and the son's actions would not cause the father grief, Joseph had forgiven his brothers and would not take vengeance against them (Genesis 50.19–21).

In Exodus we read of Moses' birth. While he was hidden among the reeds of the river, his older sister Miriam watched after him (Exodus 2.4). Through her actions, Moses was able to be nursed by his own mother before going to live as Pharaoh's grandson. When Moses was grown and returned to deliver God's people, he and Aaron, his brother, worked together to proclaim God's tidings to Pharaoh (Exodus 4.14–17). Certainly, there was that awful occurrence when Miriam and Aaron rebelled against Moses' authority, however, when God punished Miriam, Moses immediately prayed God would forgive her and remove the leprosy (Numbers 12.9–15).

According to Job 1.4–5, Job's sons had divided up the days and would demonstrate their hospitality by feeding each of their brothers and sisters on their particular day. A very interesting aspect of this is that the brothers divvied up the days. The sisters were always invited to the brothers' homes. A very interesting principle is illustrated. Brothers, your duty is to protect and provide for your sisters.

In the New Testament, the two great examples of brotherhood are James and John, and Peter and Andrew. Both sets of brothers not only grew up together but learned to work together (Matthew 4.18–22). Interestingly, it appears Peter and Andrew even lived in the same house (Mark 1.29). Perhaps, however, the greatest demonstration of love among brothers occurred between Andrew and Peter. In John 1.40–41, Andrew heard John the Baptist declare Jesus was the Messiah. The first thing he did was get Peter.

The stories of brothers and sisters fill the Bible. Examine their lives and their examples. They were not all pleasant, but each of them provides great lessons for us among our brothers and sisters.

The Golden Rule

Before we examine some dos and don'ts of the sibling relationship, we should note Jesus' Golden Rule of relationships applies nowhere more than it applies between brothers and sisters. Matthew 7.12 says, "In everything, therefore, treat people the same way you want them to treat you." Or as we commonly say, "Do unto others as you would have them do unto you."

Brothers and sisters, this should be the theme of your relationship. Do you want your siblings to exclude you from their games and activities? Then do not exclude them. Do you want your siblings to call you names? Then do not call them names. Do you want your siblings to be mean to you? Then do not be mean to them. On the other hand, do you want your siblings to treat you with kindness? Then treat them with kindness. Do you want your siblings to share with you? Then share with them. Do you want your siblings to love you? Love them.

Proverbs 18.19 says, "A brother offended is harder to be won than a strong city, and contentions are like the bars of a citadel." If you want to avoid getting in this situation, let every day in your family be governed by this Golden Rule. On it hinges all of God's law.

Some Dos and Don'ts for Siblings

To understand some of the particulars about the relationships between brothers and sisters, we will examine some of the principles taught about relationships in general. Remember what we already learned. The relationships between the Israelites and then between

Christians were often based on the understanding of how brothers and sisters were to treat one another.

Perhaps the passage that best describes the relationship between siblings is one we have already mentioned. 1 Peter 3.8–9 says, "To sum up, all of you be harmonious, sympathetic, brotherly, kind-hearted, and humble in spirit; not returning evil for evil or insult for insult, but giving a blessing instead..." Seek for harmony with your brothers and sisters. Work to get along. This will happen as you extend sympathy to them in their troubles, show them kindness and humble yourself before them. If they do not treat you as they ought, do not sink to their level. You overcome evil with good even when dealing with your brothers and sisters.

Proverbs 17.17 says, "A friend loves at all times, and a brother is born for adversity." Brothers and sisters should be there for each other in times of trouble, not to kick siblings while they are down, but to lift them up. As Ecclesiastes 4.9–12 demonstrates two are better than one, brothers and sisters need to work together to lift each other up when one has fallen.

Brothers and sisters should follow the principle of Matthew 7.1–5. Before being intent on fixing all of your brothers' and sisters' faults and flaws, you need to look to yourself first. For parents, one of the best pieces of advice I have ever heard is the "repentance bench." When brothers and sisters are fighting, have a place where they sit until they figure out what they did to contribute to the fight and what they did wrong. They are not allowed to get up until they figure it out, repent and apologize. The reality is, it doesn't matter who started it, when both are fighting, both are wrong and both need to look to themselves first.

In Zecheriah 7.9, God commanded the Israelites to "practice kindness and compassion each to his own brother." In Matthew 18.21–22, Jesus explained brothers should be forgiving, not up to seven times in a day but up to seven times seventy. Brothers and sisters need to learn mercy, compassion and forgiveness for each other. Especially as the siblings live together, hurts are going to happen. Each sibling needs to be willing to forgive.

Corresponding to that is the principle of Matthew 5.23–25. If you realize you brother or sister is upset with you, go to them quickly to resolve the matter. Do not behave immaturely waiting for them to come to you.

Deuteronomy 22.1–3 provides an interesting principle. While the NASU describes the relationship between the people in consideration as "countryman," the word is literally "brother." The text says, "You shall not see your [brother's] ox or his sheep straying away, and pay no attention to them; you shall certainly bring them back to your [brother]..." This verse and the two that follow demonstrate brothers and sisters need to respect each other's property.

Psalm 50 contains God's rebuke against the wicked as He delineates some of the sins the unrighteous committed. Vs. 20 says, "You sit and speak against your brother; you slander your own mother's son." Do not speak evil against your brother and sister. Do not badmouth your siblings behind their backs to your friends. Always speak well of them. As Matthew 5.22 demonstrates, name-calling among brothers and sisters is not tolerated by God.

In Nehemiah 5, Nehemiah heard an outcry from the poor among his people. The poor had turned to their brethren for help. Instead of helping their brethren, they took advantage of them and loaned them money at exorbitant interest rates. The loans were so expensive the brethren could not afford to pay them and were being enslaved. Nehemiah pointed out that brothers and sisters should not take advantage of each other, especially in adversity.

In Obadiah, God spoke of the nations Edom and Israel as brothers (remember they were descendents of the brothers Esau and Jacob). In Obadiah 1.12, God rebuked Edom saying, "Do not gloat over your brother's day, the day of his misfortune. And do not rejoice over the sons of Judah in the day of their destruction; Yes, do not boast in the day of their distress." Bad things will happen to our siblings. We must not gloat over them or rejoice in those days. Rather, we should be sympathetic and helpful.

Luke 12.13–15 records:

> *Someone in the crowd said to Him, "Teacher, tell my brother to divide the family inheritance with me."*

> *But He said to him, "Man, who appointed Me a judge or arbitrator over you."*
>
> *Then He said to them, "Beware, and be on your guard against every form of greed; for not even when one has an abundance does his life consist of his possessions."*

This passage demonstrates perhaps one of the most necessary principles to be remembered by brothers and sisters of all ages. We must never allow greed to come between us and our brothers and sisters. Too often an inheritance can turn brothers and sisters against each other. It would be better to hand the inheritance completely to your siblings than to allow arguing over who gets what to come between you. The family relationship is far more important than the stuff you desire to own.

Finally, Deuteronomy 13.6–8 provides a principle we must never forget. We must not let our brothers and sisters come between us and God. The text says, "If your brother, your mother's son,…entice you secretly, saying, 'Let us go and serve other gods'…you shall not yield to him or listen to him; and your eye shall not pity him, nor shall you spare or conceal him…" As close as brothers and sisters should be, our relationship with God is far more important.

Brothers and sisters should be the best of friends. Sadly, in our age segregated society, brothers and sisters typically have little to do with each other. Do not let this happen to you. Look to the principles found in scripture and make your relationship with your siblings some of the best you have.

Today's Response:

Siblings, ask each other what you can do to help each other and grow closer to one another this week. Schedule it and do it.

Point to Ponder:

How do you want your brothers and sisters to treat you? Consider it and write it down. Then work to treat them in the same way.

Today's Prayer:

Heavenly Father,

Thank You, for our brothers and sisters. We know we irritate each other some times, but we pray You will help us love each other and care for each other.

Give us strength to lift each other up when one has fallen and help us be a source of strength to each other.

Help us be sympathetic, kind-hearted and forgiving, quick to reconcile and support each other.

Forgive us for when we have not loved our brothers and sisters.

We love You Father.

In Jesus' name we pray,

Amen

Week Three Group Discussion

- What are the most important lessons you have learned this week?
- What questions do you have about what you learned this week?
- What practical improvement have you and your family made in your family lives based on what you learned this week?
- What practical advice would you give others to accomplish what you learned about this week?
- With what issues do you and your family need help or prayers based on what you learned this week?
- What do you think are the more difficult aspects of making the family roles work and how can we overcome those difficulties?
- What do you think are the keys to developing good relationships within the family between husbands and wives, parents and children, and brothers and sisters?

Week Four:

Habits of a God-Built Home

"You shall love the Lord your God with all your heart and with all your soul and with all your might. These words, which I am commanding you today, shall be on your heart. You shall teach them diligently to your sons and shall talk of them when you sit in your house and when you walk by the way and when you lie down and when you rise up. You shall bind them as a sign on your hand and they shall be as frontals on your forehead. You shall write them on the doorposts of your house and on your gates."

Deuteronomy 6.5–9

Family Worship

The Family and Congregational Worship

Aristotle said, "We are what we repeatedly do. Excellence, then, is not an act but a habit." If we want our families to excel in service to God, we have to pay attention to our habits. Just as the new man must put off old habits and put on new ones (Ephesians 4.20–24), the Christian family must put off bad habits and put on good ones. The overarching habit every family needs to develop is worship—congregationally and within the family.

Under the Old Law, God was explicit regarding the main center of worship—Jerusalem. No matter where an Israelite family lived, certain aspects of worship were to be carried out at the tabernacle, and later the temple, in the city where God placed His name.

Interestingly, as God spoke to the nation about this corporate worship, He drove home a second aspect of this worship. At times, the worshipers were to come as households.

For instance, in Deuteronomy 12.5–7 God said:

> *But you shall seek the Lord at the place which the Lord your God will choose from all your tribes, to establish His name there for His dwelling, and there you shall come. There you shall bring your burnt offerings, your sacrifices, your tithes, the contribution of your hand, your votive offerings, you freewill offerings, and the firstborn of your herd and of your flock. There also you and your households shall eat before the Lord your God, and rejoice in all your undertakings in which the Lord your God has blessed you (emphasis mine-ELC).*

This eating was a participation in the sacrifice and it occurred by household, not by individual.

Another example is Deuteronomy 15.19–20:

> *You shall consecrate to the Lord your God all the firstborn males that are born of your herd and of your flock; you shall not work with the firstborn of your herd, nor shear the firstborn of your flock. You and your household shall eat it every year before the Lord your God in the place which the Lord chooses.*

One more example is the annual observance of the Passover instituted in Exodus 12.3ff, "Speak to all the congregation of Israel, saying, 'On the tenth of this month they are each one to take a lamb for themselves, according to their fathers' households, a lamb for each household.'"

We read an example of this being fulfilled by Samuel's father, Elkanah, in 1 Samuel 1.21. "Then the man Elkanah went up with all his household to offer to the Lord the yearly sacrifice and pay his vow."

Worship, even in some of the congregational aspects, was a family issue. At times, God viewed His commands of worship to the entire congregation of Israel to be meted out by the family unit.

This same principle should be brought into our worship under the New Covenant. Obviously, if your family does not worship God, you are not precluded from congregational worship. However, even that is ideally a household or family activity. Your entire family needs to be committed to worship with a local congregation. Further, the congregational worship should not be considered as simply an occasion for Christians to get together with other individuals of their age to socialize before and after the assembly. Rather, it should be viewed as families coming together in a larger unit to glorify God together and edify one another.

I want to be very careful here because I do not want to sound like I am establishing rules in which I don't believe. However, I am concerned many congregations are getting too caught up in providing an arena for more age related segregation. The modern push for youth group mentality cannot be found in Scripture. Even worship in the congregation should be an endeavor of the family unity. Let me encourage you to give consideration to this before you make it your goal to get all the young people to consistently sit together away from their families during the congregational assemblies.

Further, if you are not yet married, consider strongly God's desire for worship to be a family activity. It is not wise or beneficial for you, or the family you want to grow, to marry someone with whom you cannot worship. I recognize there are times when this situation is inevitable (for instance, a person already married becomes a Christian). I do, however, strongly encourage you not to enter a spiritually divided marriage. The fact that it might be lawful does not make it profitable (cf. 1 Corinthians 6.12; 10.23).

The long and short of this is make the congregational assemblies a family activity. If your children live in your home, do not give them the choice of worshiping God in the assembly. Worshiping God in the congregational assembly should be an understood part of family life.

The Family and Worship at Home

For Job, worship was a family affair. Even when his children grew older, he led them in family worship. Job 1.5 says, "When the days of feasting had completed their cycle, Job would send and consecrate them, rising up early in the morning and offering burnt offerings according to the number of them all…" He would send and consecrate them. He had them involved.

Obviously, I understand the covenant of which Job was a part was far more patriarchal than our present covenant. However, we still note the importance of family worship.

Apparently, even under the Mosaic covenant, family worship was a common practice. Common enough that David was able to use family worship as a reason for not celebrating the new moon feast with Saul. 1 Samuel 20.6 says, "If your father misses me at all, then say, 'David earnestly asked leave of me to run to Bethlehem his city, because it is the yearly sacrifice there for the whole family.'" Again in 1 Samuel 20.28–29 Jonathan said, "David earnestly asked leave of me to go to Bethlehem, for he said, 'Please let me go, since our family has a sacrifice in the city, and my brother has commanded me to attend.'"

Too many people consider worship to be what we do "at church." While each and every one of us should be part of a congregation and our family should be involved as a unit in the local church, the primary place of worship should be the home. The primary unit of worshipers should be the family.

How often does your family gather for prayer? Singing? Bible study or Bible teaching? If you have never done it, I know it may sound odd, but it is necessary and it is worth it.

Acts 10.1–2 is an interesting passage. Luke was describing Cornelius, the man who would become the first Gentile convert. The text says, "Now there was a man at Caesarea named Cornelius, a centurion of what was called the Italian cohort, a devout man who feared God with all his household."

That last statement intrigues me. Fearing God seems to us like an individual emotion, not a family activity. Here was a man influenced by the Jews, yet never became one. He revered their God, giving alms to the Jews and praying to their God continually. However, his reverence was not just an individual devotion; it was a family devotion.

Since he had already made fearing God a family activity, we are not surprised to see his entire household, with relatives and close friends ready to listen and learn when Peter arrived in Acts 10.24. Many of us can say we assemble with the local church with our family. But how many can say we fear and worship God with our family?

Exodus 12.24–27 provides the great reason we must worship as families.

> *And you shall observe this event as an ordinance for you and your children forever. When you enter the land which the Lord will give you, as He has promised, you shall observe this rite. And when your children say to you, "What does this rite mean to you?" you shall say, "It is a Passover sacrifice to the Lord who passed over the houses of the sons of Israel in Egypt when He smote the Egyptians, but spared our homes."*

How much do our children learn about God by watching us worship and by participating with us? How many questions do they ask because they have seen us worshiping? "Why do you say this, Daddy?" "Why do you do that, Mommy?" Regrettably, many children never learn much about God, because they never see Dad or

Mom worshiping Him. Even fewer are ever invited to worship with Mom and Dad. Let's be the exception to this.

Some Practical Advice

Remember the story about the big rocks in Chapter 5, *Family First*? Family worship is one of those big rocks. The devil doesn't want you worshiping God with your family, especially if you have small children. He certainly doesn't want you passing on any worship habits to them. Therefore, he will rain down distractions galore to keep you from it. Worshipping God has to be scheduled and planned. If we think we will just fit it in somewhere, it will get lost in the shuffle.

Therefore, the very first practical application we need to make of this habit is make worship a scheduled fact. Think about it this way. Most people do not schedule events at 10:30 on Monday morning. Why not? Because they have jobs. In fact, most people rarely schedule anything to occur from 9 to 5, Monday through Friday because of work. Amazingly, many of us will schedule activities for Sunday without thinking twice. "God understands if we miss church just this once." However, worshipping God should hold a higher priority than work (remember Matthew 6.33). Congregational worship should simply be a scheduled reality for us and our family. Everyone should just know the scheduled services of the local congregation are worship times. Don't schedule anything else during those times.

We need to take it a step further. We also need to schedule family worship times. There are not a set number of times for this. Perhaps in your family you want to schedule a worship time every day; perhaps two or three times per week: whatever you feel is necessary for you and your family to honor and praise God together. Set the time and don't let anything get in its way. Be prepared for Satan to test you. I don't know how many times my family and I have strengthened our resolve for family worship after a regrettable hiatus. We sit down around the table, open our Bibles, start reading and the phone rings.

Turn off your ringer and let the answering machine get it. If your favorite TV show comes on at that time, set the VCR or TIVO to record. If a salesman knocks on the door, send him packing (that one's easy, you probably would have done it anyway). If your children's friends are spending the night, be an influence on them by having the family worship anyway.

While acts of worship such as the Lord's Supper and contribution are reserved for congregational worship, other aspects of worship are the same wherever you are and no matter how many are gathered together. Worship as a family the way you do with the congregation.

In your family worship, study God's word. Read it and discuss it. Devotional books are good. They might provide a springboard into topical discussions of God's word. You might even be using this book that way. However, it is not enough to simply read a devotional book. Read and study God's actual word. The advice Paul gave Timothy for the congregation applies to our families. "Give attention to the…reading of scripture" (1 Timothy 4.13).

Pray together. We will discuss this in more detail in Chapter 18. However, for now, suffice it to say our entire family needs to learn to pray. There is no better way to accomplish this than for the family to pray together. The family worship is not the congregational assembly. Every member is free to pray out loud in the family circle. Encourage and teach them to.

Sing. I know that sounds odd. However, it is an important aspect of family worship. "We couldn't carry a tune in a bucket." Do you really think God cares if you sound like an angelic choir? He simply wants you to worship. "Is anyone cheerful? He is to sing praises" (James 5.13). Sing songs of praise and worship together. "We don't know all the parts." So what! Sing the melodies. When you are with your family speak "to one another in psalms and hymns and spiritual songs, singing and making melody with your heart to the Lord" (Ephesians 5.19).

Grab a hymnal and copy some of your favorites. Take them home and sing them with your family. If you have small children, sing the children's songs with them. If you don't, sing some of the children's songs anyway. Many of the best songs with the clearest teaching are those children's songs. For instance, there's the one that teaches us Jesus loves us and we know it because the Bible tells us so. Then there is the song that tells us we need to be careful with our eyes, ears, mouths, hands and feet because God is watching us. Don't forget the one that reminds us to keep our lights shining.

We have already noticed Moses' advice In Deuteronomy 6.7, about teaching our children while we walk in the way. That is a great thought for family worship in general. However, instead of walking in the way, think about when we drive in the way. Get the Bible on tape or cd and listen to it together. Stop it and discuss what you have heard. You might even try singing together in the car.

Also from Deuteronomy 6.7, give yourself a little extra time in the morning to read or pray together. Before you go to bed, huddle up as a family for a reading and/or prayer time.

Remember, "We are what we repeatedly do. Excellence, then, is not an act but a habit." If we are going to excel before God, worship must be a habit.

Today's Response:

When will you and your family worship together this week and what will you do? Schedule it and do it.

Point to Ponder:

Why do we worship God at all? How does your answer to that first question impact what you and your family should be doing to worship together?

Today's Prayer:

Gracious God,

You are awesome beyond our possible imagination. You have blessed us so greatly. You have given us food to eat, clothes to wear, shelter to live in. You have given us family to love.

We thank You and cannot help but praise and honor You. Help us as a family to worship You. Strengthen us to glorify You together habitually. Make us worshippers who exalt Your glory continuously.

Forgive our selfishness that turns us away from Your worship and empower us to do better.

We love You Father.

Through Your Son we pray,

Amen

Family Study

The Wise Man

"The wise man built his house upon the rock…and the wise man's house stood firm." Do you remember that song from your childhood? It is based on Jesus' conclusion to His Sermon on the Mount. We find it in Matthew 7.24–27:

> *Therefore everyone who hears these words of Mine and acts on them, may be compared to a wise man who built his house on the rock. And the rain fell, and the floods came, and the winds blew and slammed against that house; and yet it did not fall, for it had been founded on the rock. Everyone who hears these words of Mine and does not act on them, will be like a foolish man who built his house on the sand. The rain fell, and the floods came, and the winds blew and slammed against that house; and it fell—and great was its fall.*

Jesus' conclusion explains the passage that is the basis for this whole study. Psalm 127.1 says, "Unless the Lord builds the house, they labor in vain who build it." The Lord builds our home by giving us the instruction manual and guiding us through it. If we want the Lord to build our home, we need to build our home on His word. When the rains, floods and winds slam against our home, it will stand.

Divided homes and divorce are rampant. Regrettably, people who claim to be Christian do not seem to fare any better than non-Christians. This can only mean one thing. Too many Christian homes are not being built upon God's word.

Psalm 119.9 says, "How can a young man keep his way pure? By keeping it according to Your word." If we want to have purity in our families, Bible study must be the foundation for our homes.

Life-Changing Bible Study

As a child, I took piano lessons. I played the drums in high school band and took trumpet as a second instrument. Now, I enjoy fiddling with the guitar. I was never really good at any of these, but I have had fun with all of them. One time, while preaching in a lectureship, I was invited into a brother's home. Noticing his guitar sitting in the corner, I picked it up and played my "big notes" version of some song or another. As the brother and I talked about our joys of playing the guitar, he gave me a piece of advice that improved my playing tremendously.

He said if I really wanted to get the hang of playing the guitar, I needed to quit putting it in its case in the closet. I needed to get a guitar stand and keep it out in the open. That way, if I had five minutes before going somewhere, I could pick it up and play a little. Certainly, there will be times when I still sit down and purposefully practice. But this unofficial practice also helps in the long run.

I think this advice applies to Bible study as well. There is the unofficial, casual getting into the Word. Then there is the intentional study. We need both. Just like that guitar, our Bibles need to be out where we can get to them easily. We ought to keep them with us as much as possible. Multiple Bibles might even help. We could have one for the house, one for work, one for the car. Keep these Bibles around. When we have an extra moment, we can pick one up and read it. I cannot stress how important this is and how important it is for this to be a family habit.

However, we also need to realize Bible reading is not the same as Bible study. Bible study is where we sit down with our Bibles and answer our questions, work out the problems and apply changes to our lives.

The Bible must never become a dusty reference book to be pulled out simply to prove a point. Nor should it ever become an ornament to be laid on the coffee table or carried to assemblies. Unless we have reached perfection, the Bible must be a manual for life change.

2 Timothy 3.14–17 demonstrates the pattern for life-changing Bible study.

> *You, however, continue in the things you have learned and become convinced of, knowing from whom you have learned them, and that from childhood you have known the sacred writings which are able to give you the wisdom that leads to salvation through faith which is in Christ Jesus.*

> *All Scripture is inspired by God and profitable for teaching, for reproof, for correction, for training in righteousness; so that the man of God may be adequate, equipped for every good work.*

In this text, Paul demonstrates three attitudes we must maintain in order to properly study the Bible.

First, we must recognize the writings as sacred. I remember one time when I was younger, attending a worship assembly with my grandfather. I laid my Bible down under the pew in front of me. My grandfather said, "Son, I never put my Bible down on the floor. That is where people's feet have been." I was heartily ashamed and asked, "Where do you put your Bible, Granddad." "I always place it on the pew next to me." With childhood innocence (or maybe not) I asked, "But Granddad, what part of their body has been there?"

The point is that the ink, pages and binding are not sacred. We should not treat our copy of the Bible as if it is some kind of holy utensil, developing rules for holding and handling it. Rather, we need to recognize that what the Bible contains is sacred. When Jesus asked the twelve if they would abandon Him, Peter responded, "Lord, to whom shall we go? You have words of eternal life" (John 6.68). The Bible is Christ's word. It contains the words of eternal life to be drunk in, meditated upon and acted on. The message it teaches is holy and we must treat it as such.

Second, we must recognize the scriptures are able to give us wisdom leading to salvation. This is an attitude about ourselves as much as it is about the Bible. We do not have all wisdom, but God's word does. When we study our Bibles, we must expect to learn something.

Third, we must recognize the Scriptures are God-breathed. When we read any other book, we may take the parts we like and discard the rest. When we are study poetry, we may learn a poem can mean different things to different people. However, when we study God's word, we must learn it means what God wants it to mean. It is His word and we must get His meaning out of it. As 2 Peter 1.20–21 shows, we are not allowed our private interpretations. Rather, we must uncover and follow God's interpretation.

Then, 2 Timothy 3.16–17 provides a four step approach to life-changing study. The Scriptures are profitable for Teaching, Reproof, Correction and Training in Righteousness.

Step 1: *Teaching*—The first step in studying any word, passage or book is to ask, "What do I learn from this study?" To answer this question we will have to ask who wrote it, to whom were they writing, does it parallel any other passages, how does it fit in the Biblical context? We will make use of Bible study tools—dictionaries, concordances and even commentaries. Whatever tools we use, we must make sure our final answer about what we have learned from the passage is what is in the Bible. Answering this question should always begin and end with getting into the Bible text.

Step 2: *Reproof*—The second question we ask in our journey of life-changing Bible study is, "Where do I fall short according to this study?" The word "reproof" means to expose error, the text is written to let us know where we are wrong. I know this is tough for us. We do not like being told we are wrong about anything. However, as we said above, unless we have attained perfection, we have to come to grips with the fact that we are falling short somewhere. It is not enough to simply learn what the passage teaches, we actually have to lay the text alongside our lives and see where we fall short.

Step 3: *Correction*—The third question we ask is, "What must I change based on this study?" The term translated "correction" connotes setting upright again what had been toppled over. If we have already answered where we fall short, the next obvious step is what must we do to correct that?

Step 4: *Training in Righteousness*—The fourth and final question we ask is, "What habits must I develop based on this study?" This is where the changing life takes place. We answer this question with actions, not pencil and paper. Training and discipline refer to the constant habit and practice of doing what is right. According to Ephesians 4.20–24, we Christians are to put off the old man and put on the new. We are to study to find the old habits and reactions that linger in our lives, remove them and replace them with new Christ-like habits and reactions. When we have taken this step, our lives have been changed by God's word and another brick has been added by God to our home.

Passing the Torch

As we pointed out in the last chapter, one of the great reasons for the family habit of worship, in all forms including Bible study, is to pass our commitment to serve God to our children. One of the great reasons for Bible study in the family is to pass the ability and the desire to study to our children.

Our children need to see us studying the Bible. Preachers especially need to think about this. It is easy for us to do all our study at the office and our children never know what it means for us to "go to work." They need to see us studying.

Also, we need to actually study with our kids. That will help them develop the know-how and the habit. Understand that reading a quick Bible story and answering a few true false, multiple choice or fill-in-the-blank questions to prepare for a Bible class is not really study.

We could perhaps write an entire book on how to pass this torch to our children. However, for our purposes let me offer two principles.

Principle #1—*Use the Bible.* "Veggie Tales" and "Pop-up books" have their place, but they are not the Bible. Read the Bible to them. Make it interesting by providing Bible characters' voices. Make it fun by having them act it out. But read from the Bible. Further, answer their questions by actually going to the Bible. Don't just tell them what you know is the answer, quote the passage that teaches it or even take them to it. As they get older, show them how to use dictionaries and concordances that they might be able to look up the answer themselves. Use the Bible to correct behavioral problems and to praise behavioral successes. If they lie, correct them with Ephesians 4.25 or Revelation 21.8. When they show respect and obey you properly, praise them with Ephesians 6.1–3. Finally, use the Bible by having your children memorize it. "Your word I have treasured [hidden] in my heart, that I may not sin against You" (Psalm 119.11).

Principle #2—*Go from milk to meat.* Hebrews 5.11–14 demonstrates Bible learning is a growth process. Just as infants start their nutritional lives on milk and then gradually progress to solid food, we should do the same with spiritual food for our children. We shouldn't expect our four-year olds or fourteen-year olds to understand all the weighty matters of God's word. However, we should expect our fourteen-year old to be farther along than his younger siblings. We should start off with our children in the youngest years by giving them "hooks" on which to hang information. By that, I mean read them Bible stories. Let them learn lists like the books of the Bible, Judges, Kings, Apostles, Fruit of the Spirit, etc. They won't understand them. But as they grow and hear more, these tidbits of information will provide something akin to filing cabinets in which to store new information. Then move to getting them to read the Bible stories on their own and tell you what happened. As they get in their pre-teen years, you can typically start working with them on the "Why" of the Bible. Have them think about why God called Abraham or why Jesus had to come into the world. The final key is to help them learn to express what they have learned. They need to be able to reasonably and concisely explain what they believe and why. We are not trying to turn all of our children into preachers, just people who are able to give an answer for the hope that lies within them (1 Peter 3.15).

We are what we repeatedly do. Let's be disciples, students of Christ's word. Develop the habit of family Bible study and watch your home be built by the Lord.

Today's Response:

What book in the Bible will you and your family start studying this week? How much will you cover each day? When will you start?

Point to Ponder:

What did you learn about Bible study from 2 Timothy 3.14–17?

____

____

____

Where do you and your family fall short when it comes to Bible study?

____

____

What corrections do you need to make?

____

____

What habits do you need to develop?

____

____

____

Today's Prayer:

Dear Heavenly Father,

Thank You so much for Your Word that is a lamp to our feet and a light to our path. Forgive us when we have not followed it as we ought.

Strengthen our family to study Your Word more diligently and apply Your Word more accurately. Help us understand, give us wisdom and enlightenment that we may truly know Your power and Your grace.

Help us, Lord, pass Your Word on to our children, that they may grow to be Your faithful servants.

We love You Father.

By Your Son's authority we pray,

Amen

Family Prayer

Prayer Leaders

1 Thessalonians 5.17 says, "Pray without ceasing." If "we are what we repeatedly do," we ought to be prayers. Certainly, prayer is part of the family habit of worship. However, like Bible study, we need to examine this habit more closely, looking at each family member's involvement in prayer.

As Ephesians 5.22–24 says, husbands and fathers are the head of the home. We are responsible, then, to answer this question: How is our family's prayer life? We must not talk about how our wives won't cooperate with us. We must not vacillate using our children's schedule as an excuse. We must consider our family's prayer life.

Do we pray more than at meals and a quick, "Now I lay me down to sleep..." at bedtime? Do we even do that? Husbands, we are at war! Ephesians 6.10–13, explains the battle. We are fighting against hellish forces of the devil himself and they are not just attacking our society in general, they are attacking our families in specific. We can only overcome if we access God and His power through prayer. We have to set the vision. We have to lay out the battle plan. We have to lead our family in prayer.

Our role in prayer should mirror Jesus' role in prayer for the church (cf. Ephesians 5.23). What does Jesus do in prayer for the church?

Romans 8.34 says, "Christ Jesus is He who died, yes who rather was raised, who is at the right hand of God, who also intercedes for us." Hebrews 7.25 says, "Therefore He is able also to save forever those who draw near to God through Him, since He always lives to make intercession for them." Jesus intercedes for His church. We need to intercede for our families. How much time do we spend praying on our family's behalf? How many prayers do we offer up for our wives or our children? When we do offer up prayers are we specific or do we just pray, "Lord please bless my wife and kids"? Do we pray for our wives' and children's needs and desires or do we actually pray for our own—"Lord, please help my wife be more submissive, less emotional and make her get off my back about the cluttered garage"? Selfishness has no place in prayer, especially not under the guise of intercession.

In Luke 11.1–13, Jesus taught His disciples, and through them His church, to pray. Do we teach our families to pray? Interestingly, Jesus taught the disciples because the disciples saw something in His prayer life worth learning. Would our family ever ask us how to pray based on the example we have set? We must teach our families by example. We should pray with them. They should hear us praise God, give thanks, confess sin and make supplication. We must teach them by instruction. Show them what the Bible says about prayer. Study the Bible's prayers with them.

Finally, husbands, if we are going to lead our family in prayer, we have to treat our family properly. 1 Peter 3.7 says, "...and show her honor as a fellow heir of the grace of life, so that your prayers will not be hindered." If we mistreat our family, especially our wives, our prayers will not be profitable. We must lead in prayer and we must make our prayers worthwhile by living properly in our family.

Prayer Partners

As we pointed out earlier, the overarching principle of the wife's role in the family is to be a suitable helper (Genesis 2.18). Proverbs 31.12 said you should do good to your husband all the days of your life. The greatest good you can ever do him and the greatest help you can ever offer is prayer. Pray with him; pray for him.

Keep Psalm 127.1 in mind. "Unless the Lord builds the house, they labor in vain who build it." And then vs. 2, "It is vain for you to rise up early, to retire late, to eat the bread of painful labors; for He gives to His beloved even in his sleep." So many wives do so much for their families. They work countless hours to provide materially for the family. They come home, too often to unappreciative husbands and children, to cook and clean. They run their kids around to all kinds of events. They go over their kids' homework and Bible class lessons. They wash and iron clothes. They burn the candle at both ends to get all the work done, rising early and retiring late. But how many make any of it worthwhile by inviting God into their families through prayer?

Sadly, Satan has overcome the prayer lives of many women by getting them to compete with their husbands. Too often, husbands and wives compete for the prize of who adds the most, does the most, sacrifices the most and has the toughest time. Satan fosters this infighting, because if we are attacking each other, we have little time to mount prayerful attacks on him. Competition is a big hindrance to prayer in the home. Wives, when you view your husband as competition, you view him as the enemy. It's hard to intercede for the good of the enemy. Of course, if you have gotten to that point in your family, remember Matthew 5.44: "But I say to you, love your enemies and pray for those who persecute you." You are to pray for your husband, even if he is your enemy. However, wouldn't it be easier if you brought down the walls of competition and viewed him as your partner? I know many wives have husbands who do not view the marriage as a partnership. Instead of trying to knock him down a notch or two by competing with him, why not start the partnering process by praying for him and offering to pray with him?

If you want to pray properly in your home, you will first have to allow Peter's advice in 1 Peter 3.3–4 to sink in:

> *Your adornment must not be merely external—braiding the hair, and wearing gold jewelry, or putting on dresses; but let it be the hidden person of the heart, with the imperishable quality of a gentle and quiet spirit, which is precious in the sight of God.*

This does not mean you have to change your personality. It simply means you have to remember you are a partner to your husband. To truly accomplish that, you are going to have to value what God values, think what God thinks and want what God wants. You have to let your life and your family be God's instruments to work in His world. This is the crux of successful prayer. Prayer only works when we line up with God in our values, thoughts, desires, words and actions.

If your husband simply is not and will not be the prayer leader he is supposed to be, remember 1 Peter 3.1–2:

> *In the same way, you wives, be submissive to your own husbands so that even if any of them are disobedient to the word, they may be won without a word by the behavior of their wives, as they observe your chaste and respectful behavior.*

Continue to conduct yourself in discreet submission. Continue praying for your husband. Pray for yourself that you might be the wife you know you ought to be, even when he is making it hard for you. Pray for your husband in front of your children and get your children to pray for him. Thank God for your husband and the aspects of his life that are praiseworthy; and do so in front of your children. Finally, never belittle your husband because he is not what he ought to be. Simply pray for him and strive to complement him, using your strengths to make up for his weaknesses.

In such a manner, wives, will you be the wise women who build up their homes (Proverbs 14.1).

Obedient Prayers

Regrettably, we often view prayer as an adult activity. At least we view serious prayer that way. Sure, we will do the night-night prayers and a simple "Saying Grace" before meals with the kids, but the most helpful way to make adults strong prayers is to get them started while they are children.

Kids, do not wait until you leave home to start praying seriously. Do not wait until you are "old enough." Start praying right now. The place you need to start is in seeking help to fulfill your role as obedient and honoring children. You have to remember Ephesians 6.1–2 governs everything you do, even your prayers. "Children, obey your parents in the Lord, for this is right. Honor your father and mother…"

Do this in prayer. Pray for strength from God to obey and honor your parents. Honor your parents in prayer by praying for them. Whether you like to read this or not, raising you is not easy. Your parents believe it is the toughest thing they have to do. They live in constant fear that they are doing it incorrectly. Pray for them to have wisdom to raise you properly. Further, you should thank

God profusely for your parents, even with all their faults. They feed you, they clothe you, they send you to school, they bring you to worship. They deserve your prayers. But even if they don't deserve them, they need them.

"We are what we repeatedly do." Are we prayers? How much place does prayer have in our family? Remember, if God is not involved in building our homes, all the other stuff we do is in vain. God will not be involved unless we invite Him in through prayer.

Today's Response:

Now that you have read through this chapter, stop and pray for your family. If you read this chapter with your family, pray together.

How often do you think your family should pray together? When will your family pray together? Schedule it and do it.

Point to Ponder:

Matthew 7.7–11 says God gives good gifts to those who ask Him. What kinds of blessings has your family received because you asked? What kinds of blessings have you missed because you have not asked?

Today's Prayer:

Holy God and Father in Heaven,

Thank You for letting us pray to You. We confess our sins and ask that You forgive us, allowing us into Your presence to bring our praise and our petitions.

Strengthen our family to glorify You constantly through prayer, to pray without ceasing, rejoicing always and giving thanks in everything.

Be with each family member that we will all fill our roles in the family and in prayer. Help us give You the glory You deserve.

We love You Father.

Through Jesus we pray,

Amen

Wisdom and Instruction

Discipline and Instruction

We have already learned the parents' responsibilities. Ephesians 6.4 says, "Fathers, do not provoke your children to anger, but bring them up in the discipline and instruction of the Lord."

If we want our family to pursue excellence in serving the Lord and if we want that to continue on after we are gone, we parents have to pass on discipline and instruction. This teaching has to be a habit.

By habit, I do not mean we have to set up some kind of daily class lesson with our kids to give them wisdom and instruction. Rather, we must keep our eyes open for opportunities to pass on the lessons of life. Not only keep our eyes open, but work to make opportunities.

Maya Angelou tells a story of her grandmother. When Angelou was a child working in her grandmother's store in Stamps, Arkansas, her grandmother would incite opportunities to teach "sister." Angelou recounts that when someone known as a whiner came into the store, her grandmother would ask them how they were doing. Of course, they would go on about how bad everything was. This hurt, that hurt, this was negative and that was bad. When the complainer left, her grandmother would call her in front of her and ask, "Did you hear what Brother such-and-such or Sister much-to-do said?" Angelou would nod and her grandmother would continue, "Sister, there are people who went to sleep all over the world last night, poor and rich and white and black, but they will never wake again. And those dead folks would give anything, anything at all for just five minutes of this weather that person was grumbling about. So you watch yourself about complaining, Sister. What you're supposed to do when you don't like a thing is change it. If you can't change it, change the way you think about it. Don't complain."

Angelou's grandmother looked for opportunities and even made opportunities to pass wisdom on to her granddaughter. That is making wisdom and instruction a habit in the family.

But what issues of wisdom and instruction should we pass on to our children? The book of Proverbs provides a great pattern for what to pass on. Proverbs 1.8 says, "Hear, my son, your father's instruction and do not forsake your mother's teaching." The entirety of this book is wisdom passed from parent to child. We can learn a lot about what to teach our children from it.

If you are a parent, you should read it repeatedly. Not only will it provide you with great wisdom, it will provide you with insight for teaching your children. A great plan someone passed on to me about Proverbs is to read a chapter every day. Proverbs has 31 chapters and our months are 30 to 31 days. Imagine how much wisdom would sink in if we read the book 12 times every year. Obviously, I am not going to include the entire book here. But we will notice some of the general topics we need to pass on to our children habitually.

A Relationship with God

Trust in the Lord with all your heart
And do not lean on your own understanding.
In all your ways acknowledge Him,
And he will make your paths straight.
Do not be wise in your own eyes;
Fear the Lord and turn away from evil
It will be healing to your body
And refreshment to your bones.
Honor the Lord from your wealth
And from the first of all your produce;
So your barns will be filled with plenty
And your vats will overflow with new wine.
My son, do not reject the discipline of the Lord
Or loathe His reproof,

For whom the Lord loves He reproves,
Even as a father corrects the son in whom he delights.
Proverbs 3.5–12

This passage contains the keys we must pass on to our children regarding their developing relationship with God. Do not wait until your children are teenagers to start working on this. Start them young. Just as you started teaching them to love you and that you loved them from the moment they came into the world, you need to teach them to love God and that He loves them as well.

We must teach our children to trust God, even when they don't understand why He has commanded something. We must do things His way, trusting His way is the right way. As Isaiah 55.8–9 says, His ways and thoughts are higher than ours. We must simply trust Him.

We must teach our children to acknowledge God in all their ways. If we live in a house, have a car, have clothes to wear and food to eat, we need to acknowledge God's grace in that. Without God's mercy we could have none of these things. If we have a job, we must learn to recognize the gift from the Lord. He is the one who has given us strength to live, move and have our very being (Acts 17.28). We must acknowledge Him and thank Him. We must teach our children to turn to God for strength to accomplish any endeavor and when it is accomplished to turn to Him in thanks.

We must teach our children to recognize God's wisdom. We must teach our children to recognize the fruits of God's wisdom. "The wisdom from above is first pure, then peaceable, gentle, reasonable, full of mercy and good fruits, unwavering, without hypocrisy" (James 3.17). We must teach our children that we gain God's wisdom through God's word. "You, however, continue in the things you have learned… that from childhood you have known the sacred writings which are able to give you the wisdom that leads to salvation through faith which is in Christ Jesus" (2 Timothy 3.14–15).

We must teach our children to fear God. Yes, I know this is not popular today. However, it is still something we and our children must learn. Granted, God is not some cosmic lightening bolt waiting for us to mess up in order to blast us. However, He is a jealous God who expects obedience from His children. "Behold then the kindness and severity of God; to those who fell, severity, but to you, God's kindness, if you continue in His kindness; otherwise you will be cut off" (Romans 11.22).

We must teach our children to honor God from the best of their wealth. Do you give your kids an allowance? Have them determine a portion to contribute to the Lord's work. Did they receive a birthday check from grandma? Help them see they should thank God for His merciful benevolence to them. Did they help clean up a neighbor's yard and get paid? Teach them to give a portion to the Lord. Do not think they will just see you giving and know what to do once they have grown up. Teach them by having them start giving to the Lord while they are young. "…God loves a cheerful giver" (2 Corinthians 9.7).

Finally, we must teach them to accept the Lord's discipline. The Lord disciplines the children He loves. "All discipline for the moment seems not to be joyful, but sorrowful; yet to those who have been trained by it, afterwards it yields the peaceful fruit of righteousness" (Hebrews 12.11).

Relationships with Others

We must teach our children to live properly in all their relationships, whether family, community or congregation.

Perhaps the overarching principle for positive interpersonal relationships is found in Proverbs 3.3–4. "Do not let kindness and truth leave you; bind them around your neck, write them on the tablet of your heart. So you will find favor and good repute in the sight of God and man." Kindness and honesty are the two keys to good relationships. The Golden Rule should be pursued by all. "In everything, therefore, treat people the same way you want them to treat you" (Matthew 7.12).

As Ephesians 4 demonstrates, the new man must put on these qualities: "Therefore, laying aside falsehood, speak truth each one of you with his neighbor…Be kind to one another, tender-hearted, forgiving each other, just as God in Christ also has forgiven you" (Ephesians 4.25, 32). 1 Peter 3.8–9 says, "To sum up, all of you be harmonious, sympathetic, brotherly, kindhearted, and humble in spirit; not returning evil for evil or insult for insult, but giving a blessing instead..."

We must teach our children as early as possible not to give way to peer pressure. As Proverbs 1.10, 15 says, "My son, if sinners entice you, do not consent...My son, do not walk in the way with them. Keep your feet from their path..." Of course, to teach this to our children, we must also be busy teaching them what is right and wrong. We must teach our children to be the influencers and not the influenced. Further, as we have already learned to teach them that they must fear God, we should teach them not to fear those who would pressure us to turn from God. The worst they can do is kill us. "Do not fear those who kill the body but are unable to kill the soul; but rather fear Him who is able to destroy both soul and body in hell" (Matthew 10.28).

Our children have already learned in chapter 14 to be obedient. However, we have to understand that children do not come out of the womb naturally programmed to obey. As Proverbs 6.20–22 demonstrates, they have to be taught to obey:

> *My son, observe the commandment of your father*
> *And do not forsake the teaching of your mother;*
> *Bind them continually on your heart;*
> *Tie them around you neck.*
> *When you walk about, they will guide you;*
> *When you sleep, they will watch over you;*
> *And when you awake, they will talk to you.*

I saw a great sign in front of a church building the other day. It said, "The time to teach obedience is in the playpen, not the state pen." Teaching our children to obey when they are little is far easier than thinking they are too young to be expected to obey and then waiting until they are old enough to talk back about it. Start young. Teach them to obey you. Doing so will help you teach them the next key regarding relationships in our world.

We need to teach our children to respect those in authority. Proverbs 24.21 says, "My son, fear the Lord and the king..." While the proverbialist specifically says "king," I believe the point is about authority—whether that authority is in the home, in the church or in the civil government.

Hebrews 13.17 says, "Obey your leaders and submit to them, for they keep watch over your souls…" Certainly, the first application of that verse is within the church. However, the principle is the same for all walks of life. We must learn and teach our children to submit to those in authority. We must teach our children to respect us, their parents. We must also teach them to respect their teachers at school, employers at work, policeman in the community, elders and teachers in the church. Further, we should teach them to respect their elders in general. This teaching is lost in our society. Children naturally have a tendency to believe if someone is not their mother or father, they do not have to listen to or respect them. It is a travesty when parents support this. Consider the story of Elisha and the forty-two boys in 2 Kings 23:

> *Then [Elisha] went up from there to Bethel; and as he was going up by the way, young lads came out from the city and mocked him and said to him, "Go up, you baldhead; go up, you baldhead!" When he looked behind him and saw them, he cursed them in the name of the Lord. Then two female bears came out of the woods and tore up forty-two lads of their number.*

As Leviticus 19.32 taught, we should teach our children to "rise up before the grayheaded and honor the aged."

Matters of Life

Finally, we need to teach our children some general principles for living wisely and righteously in this world. I will simply give you a list of passages in Proverbs that provide some main topics to help our children grow up and live wisely.

According to Proverbs 4.23–24, our children must learn to watch their thoughts and their words. "Watch over your heart with all diligence, for from it flow the springs of life. Put away from you a deceitful mouth and put devious speech far from you." They must learn to watch what goes into and what lingers in their hearts. Further, they must learn to measure their words that they may bring grace to those who hear them, building them up and not tearing them down (cf. Ephesians 4.29).

Proverbs 5.1–23 demonstrates we must teach our children the proper context in which to fulfill sexual desire. Further, we must warn our children and prepare them for the temptations the world holds regarding these issues, helping them develop a plan to overcome.

Proverbs 6.1–3 is one of several passages in the book that talk about dealing with money. We live in a material world. We cannot escape money. Therefore, we must teach our children how to use it wisely, governing money instead of letting money govern them.

Proverbs 6.6–11 and 10.5 both teach about work and discipline. "Go to the ant, O sluggard, observe her ways and be wise..." "He who gathers in summer is a son who acts wisely, but he who sleeps in harvest is a son who acts shamefully." We must teach our children a positive and beneficial work ethic. There is far too much entitlement mentality in our society. We must teach Paul's words in 2 Thessalonians 3.10, "If anyone is not willing to work, then he is not to eat."

We must teach our children to control their physical passions, controlling their hunger and not living in excess. Proverbs 23.20–21 says, "Do not be with heavy drinkers of wine, or with gluttonous eaters of meat; for the heavy drinker and the glutton will come to poverty, and drowsiness will clothe one with rags." Instead of eating and drinking to excess, allowing our stomachs to control us, we should govern our bodies and eat when it is appropriate. As Ecclesiastes 10.16–17 says, "Woe to you, O land, whose king is a lad and whose princes feast in the morning. Blessed are you, O land, whose king is of nobility and whose princes eat at the appropriate time—for strength and not for drunkenness." As we commonly say, "We should eat to live, not live to eat."

Considering the overpowering marketing regarding beer and liquor in our society, we need to teach our children the truth regarding alcohol. Proverbs 23.31 says, "Do not look on the wine when it is red, when it sparkles in the cup, when it goes down smoothly; at the last it bites like a serpent and stings like a viper." Proverbs 31.4 says, "It is not for kings to drink wine, or for rulers to desire strong drink." Teach them to stay away from it. It is a mocker and a brawler, those who are misled by it are fools (Proverbs 20.1).

Finally, Proverbs 31.10–31 demonstrates we need to teach our children what kind of mate to look for. Notice the chapter is addressed to Lemuel and is written by his mother (Lemuel is most likely a poetic name for Solomon). She was not writing to tell women how to be wives. She was writing to tell her son what kind of woman to marry. However, let's keep in mind the rest of Proverbs was written to tell that son what kind of man to be. Therefore, we need to teach our children what kind of mate to look for and what kind of mate to be.

*****

Wisdom and instruction need to be a habit in our homes. Proverbs 17.21 says, "He who sires a fool does so to his sorrow, and the father of a fool has no joy." This passage is not saying if we are unlucky and happen to end up with a fool for a child we will be sorry. The point is if we don't make wisdom and instruction a habit in our home, our kids will end up being fools. Let's not raise any fools.

Today's Response:

Consider the issues of wisdom and instruction that need to be passed on to your children. Prioritize them. Which ones do you need to start working on right now with your children? What can you do this week to pass that wisdom and instruction on to them?

Point to Ponder:

One of the best ways to teach is to exemplify the lesson being taught. Among the aspects of wisdom discussed in this chapter, which ones do you need to work on? How can you work on them?

Today's Prayer:

All-wise Father,

We are in awe of Your wisdom. You set at naught the wisdom of this world and demonstrate that the wise in the world are but fools.

Help us, Father, be wise in Your wisdom and Your ways, which are higher than ours. Help us pass that wisdom and instruction on to our children. We recognize wisdom will guide us in this world, helping us be Your effective servants. Forgive us when we have turned our backs on Your wisdom and help us always return to it.

We love You Father.

Through Your Son we pray,

Amen

Hospitality

A Dying American Habit

> Communal socializing also appears to be on the way out. Putnam finds that Americans in 1997 were entertaining friends and acquaintances at home 40 percent less often than in 1975, attending club meetings nearly 60 percent less often, and giving half as many dinner parties. Families are also eating together less often. In 1975, 50 percent of married Americans agreed that "our whole family usually eats dinner together"; in 1997 only 34 percent did. When we add the increasing number of single people living by themselves, "dining alone" may have doubled in the past quarter century. What we are doing more of, to replace this communal activity, is watching TV, renting videos, Web surfing and working on our home computers.
>
> *David G. Myers, The American Paradox, Yale Univ. Press, New Haven, 2000, p. 179*

Regrettably, the dying of this American habit seems to be mirrored in the church. One of the defining aspects of the first local church was hospitality. Acts 2.46 described those very first Christians saying, "Day by day continuing with one mind in the temple and breaking bread from house to house, they were taking their meals together with gladness and sincerity of heart…" The church did not have to build a fellowship hall or set up a group program, the Christians just got together, being hospitable and providing for one another.

Myers went on to explain what he believes is the reason for diminishing hospitality and togetherness in America:

> Hanging in the societal balance, on one side is our valuing of self-fulfillment—insistence on our rights, cherishing

> personal freedom, pursuit of passion and pleasure. On the other side hangs our valuing of commitments—our sense of responsibility, our regarding permanence as a virtue, our believing that love is not just a feeling but a binding obligation. Over time, the balance has shifted toward prizing fulfillment over commitment, rights over responsibilities, wants over oughts.
>
> *Myers, p. 182*

It is a sad commentary on our society. Yet, Myers's assessment implies exactly why hospitality is such an important habit for a family to develop. Christian families are to be focused on commitment, not fulfillment; responsibilities, not rights; oughts, not wants. We must be different from the world around us (cf. Romans 12.2).

Romans 12.9–13 says, "Let love be without hypocrisy...Be devoted to one another in brotherly love, give preference to one another in honor...contributing to the needs of the saints, practicing hospitality." We must not let this love die in our families.

Hospitality: What Is It?

Webster's defines "hospitality" as "the friendly reception and treatment of guests or strangers" and "the quality or disposition of receiving and treating guests and strangers in a warm, friendly, and generous way." Vine, in his dictionary of New Testament words, defines it as simply "loving strangers." Strong, in his enhanced lexicon, says the word in the Greek comes from two words that together literally mean "friend to strangers."

Hospitality, therefore, means far more than simply having a meal with someone. Hospitality means receiving someone in a warm and friendly manner, being generous toward others, having familiar association with even strangers and being a companion to these.

Consider some amazing demonstrations of hospitality in Acts 16. Lydia, the first European convert, immediately invited Paul and Silas into her home when she became a Christian in Acts 16.15, saying, "If you have judged me to be faithful to the Lord, come into my house and stay." Further, it appears that Lydia opened her home to all the brethren in Acts 16.40. The jailer, when he was converted brought Paul and Silas into his home and provided for their physical needs, cleaning the wounds from their unlawful beating and feeding them in Acts 16.33–34.

Talking about hospitality as a habit of a God-built home may seem odd in the context of the other habits—all of which have to do with the personal spirituality of the family members. However, we have to learn that the habits of a God-built home are not all internally focused.

When we enter Christ we put on the new man. Ephesians 4.28 says about the new man, "He who steals must steal no longer; but rather he must labor…so that he will have something to share with one who has need." God has given our family blessings not so we can horde them, but so we might be a blessing to others. One blessing to others is hospitality.

Hospitality: Why Is It Important?

Obviously, hospitality is important simply because God commanded it. We have already seen Romans 12.13 above. Did you notice that hospitality was part of loving without hypocrisy? We know from 1 Corinthians 13.1–3 that we can do all sorts of seemingly great things, but if we do not have love, we are no more than noisy gongs or clanging cymbals. We are nothing and our actions profit us nothing.

1 Peter 4.7–9 says, "The end of all things is near; therefore…be hospitable to one another..." Peter linked hospitality to preparing for judgment. The parable of judgment in Matthew 25.31–46 corresponds. Frankly, this parable frightens me. It explains that we may get the doctrines surrounding salvation, worship, congregational organization, theology and eschatology right, but if we don't get the practice of hospitality right, we will be shunted off to the left with the goats, because, "to the extent that you did it to one of these brothers of Mine, even the least of them, you did it to Me… to the extent that you did not do it to one of the least of these, you did not do it to Me."

The story is told of a man who had a vision on a Saturday evening. He saw Jesus in his dream. Jesus told the man He would be visiting the man's congregation the next day. The man was to prepare a meal for Jesus because He would come home with him. The man told his wife and kids. They immediately got up and cleaned the house and went back to bed very late. The man and his wife got up early and prepared a meal fit for a king and left it timing in the oven so it would be ready as soon as they got home. They didn't want the Lord to have to wait even one minute. The table was set, the house was spotless, the kids were in their absolute "Sunday best." They left for worship, slightly late, but nonetheless excited that they would be meeting and eating with Jesus in just a couple of hours.

When they arrived, the family spent most of their time looking for Jesus, but they did not see anyone they thought remotely might be Him. They were so intent on looking for Jesus they barely paid attention to anything that happened in their classes or the assembly. Having gone through the whole service without seeing Jesus, they heard the closing statements as the preacher told the congregation that one of the brothers had been laid off. The family was struggling and needed all the help they could get. The man and his wife were disappointed, but decided it would be pointless to let their meal fit for a king go to waste. They invited the newly unemployed brother and his family over for lunch. They enjoyed the lunch and figured out some ways to help the family and make some contacts for the brother to get a new job.

The next Saturday afternoon, the man was napping and had another dream. Jesus was there and the man said, "Lord, we prepared for You, we looked for You, but we didn't see You." To which Jesus responded, "I was there, you must have missed Me. However, I am planning to visit your congregation again tomorrow. Please, be ready for Me to eat with you." The man awoke and the family repeated their preparations just as the week before. However, once again, despite their searching, they did not see Jesus. The only special visitor was an evangelist from a foreign country whom the congregation had supported financially for years. He was giving a report and discussed the numerous opportunities for service in his homeland. Once again, the man and his wife were disappointed, but didn't want all of their preparations to be for naught. They invited the preacher and his wife over for lunch. They learned a great deal about evangelism and about the life of Christians in foreign lands. They even learned a way for them to help out specifically.

By the end of that week, they had nearly overcome their disappointment. On the next Saturday, the man had another vision. There was Jesus again. The man repeated his complaint, "Lord, we prepared for you, we looked for You, but we didn't see You." Jesus replied again, "I was there, you must have missed Me. However, I am going to be visiting one more time with you tomorrow. Please, be prepared one more time." Though not quite as eager about it, the whole family pitched in thinking, "Third time's the charm." Yet, once again, they didn't see Jesus. However, not wanting to waste their meal, they decided to invite another brother and his kids over for lunch. The man's wife had been in the hospital for several days. They thought it would be good for him not to have to worry about how to feed the kids before they went on to the hospital to sit with her. It was a pleasant lunch and the hosts even offered to keep the kids and sit with the man's wife in the hospital.

That night, the man saw Jesus in his dreams again. He complained, "Lord, we have prepared and looked for You three weeks in a row, but you haven't shown up even once. Why did You do this to us?" As I am sure you have already guessed, Jesus replied, "I was there and I enjoyed your hospitality these three weeks in a row. When you loved the family whose husband and father had been laid off, you loved Me. When you helped My servant and spokesman who proclaims the gospel in the foreign land, you helped Me. When you showed hospitality and encouragement to your brother whose wife was sick, you showed it to Me."

Granted, I do not believe you will have visions guiding you to be prepared for hospitality. However, I do believe the principle taught in Hebrews 13.2, "Do not neglect to show hospitality to strangers, for by this some have entertained angels without knowing it." We must not close the doors of our families and our blessings to our brethren, lest we find we have closed the door of our families to Jesus Himself.

Hospitality: How and to Whom?

Read 1 Peter 4.9 again. "Be hospitable to one another without complaint." Strong's Enhanced Lexicon says the word translated "complaint" means "a secret debate" or "a secret displeasure not openly avowed." We are to practice hospitality with a cheerful and willing heart. We should not be grumbling about the inconvenience or the cost. We should simply be happy to share our blessings with others. That is, after all, the reason God has blessed us.

Galatians 6.9–10 says, "Let us not lose heart in doing good, for in due time we will reap if we do not grow weary. So then, while we have opportunity, let us do good to all people, and especially to those who are of the household of faith." This verse gives some insight in the how and who of hospitality. First, we must practice hospitality without growing weary. Let's face it, hospitality takes work. We may get tired of this output. We must not. Second, we see we have a special obligation to do good, including hospitality, to our brethren. Our bond in Christ makes us responsible to one another. However, we should also take opportunity to be a blessing to those who are not Christians. Friends, family, schoolmates, co-workers and others should enjoy our hospitality as we have opportunity to do them good.

Keep in mind Hebrews 13.2. Remember it says, "Do not neglect to show hospitality to strangers..." This passage is in the context of loving brethren. Lest someone blow what I am saying out of proportion, this passage does not obligate us to pick up strange hitchhikers on the highways. But it does point out we have a bond to brethren, even ones we do not know. Traveling brethren, brethren who have newly moved, new Christians may all be strangers to us. However, that bond in Christ should overcome our discomfort and prompt us to share our blessings with them, associating with them as friends.

We must also recognize true hospitality does not keep score. In Luke 14.12–14, Jesus taught, "When you give a reception, invite the poor, the crippled, the lame, the blind, and you will be blessed, since they do not have the means to repay you; for you will be repaid at the resurrection of the righteous." Jesus' point was not to restrict us from ever being hospitable to those who might return the generosity. Rather, His point was that we ought to be the most hospitable to those who most need it. If we are only being hospitable because we are hoping for some return in payment for our generosity, it is does us no eternal good. Hospitality is about doing good to others, not trying to do good to ourselves. Many are happy to be hospitable to the rich and powerful, because they hope to gain some greater benefit. However, we receive the greatest eternal benefit when we are being a blessing to others simply to be a blessing to them.

There is one limitation on our hospitality. 2 Thessalonians 3.10 says, "...if anyone is not willing to work, then he is not to eat, either." We are not to enable laziness or undisciplined lives by providing the needs of those who refuse to work. This does not refer to those unable to work, but those who will not.

Hospitality is a dying habit in our society. We must not let it die out in our families. A home built by the Lord is a home that shares the love and spreads the blessing.

Today's Response:

How and to whom can you show hospitality this week? Schedule it and do it.

Point to Ponder:

If God were to judge you today based on your hospitality (Matthew 25.31–46), how would you fare? What improvements can you and your family make?

Today's Prayer:

Benevolent Father,

You have blessed us far more than we deserve. We thank You and praise You for Your grace and mercy. We thank You for the food we eat, the homes in which we live, the clothes we wear, the cars we drive. We are truly blessed.

Father, please strengthen us to bless others through the blessings You have granted us. Please enable us with opportunities and resources to be Your blessing in the lives of others.

We love You Father.

Through Your Son we pray,

Amen

Week Four Group Discussion

- What are the most important lessons you have learned this week?
- What questions do you have about what you learned this week?
- What practical improvement have you and your family made in your family lives based on what you learned this week?
- What practical advice would you give others to accomplish what you learned about this week?
- With what issues do you and your family need help or prayers based on what you learned this week?
- What are some negative habits you believe hinder families from being built by the Lord?
- What other habits would you suggest for families that desire to let the Lord build their homes?

Week Five:

Our Family and God's Family

"Paul, a prisoner of Christ Jesus, and Timothy our brother, To Philemon our beloved brother and fellow worker, and to Apphia our sister, and to Archippus our fellow soldier, and to the church in your house: Grace to you and peace from God our Father and the Lord Jesus Christ."

Philemon 1–3

Just Like Family

Not a Country Club

Why did you pick the local congregation you are attending? Sadly, most people today shop churches like they are shopping country clubs. "What do you have to offer me?" "What services do you provide?" "How many people my age attend here?" "What are the dues?"

The local church, while it provides a great deal for us, is not a country club. We must understand this, because usually the people who shop churches like country clubs, are members of the local congregation in the same way they are of the local country club. They come in when they want to be served. They pay their dues every now and then. They complain about what they don't like. They leave when things don't go their way.

The congregation is a community of like-minded people who have agreed to assemble regularly, working together for a common purpose, under a common leadership, using a common treasury. But even that "doctrinal" definition doesn't get to the heart of what the local church is. If you want to see the heart of a great congregation, look at Acts 4.32–35:

> *And the congregation of those who believed were of one heart and soul; and not one of them claimed that anything belonging to him was his own, but all things were common property to them. And with great power the apostles were giving testimony to the resurrection of the Lord Jesus, and abundant grace was upon them all. For there was not a needy person among them, for all who were owners of land or houses would sell them and bring the proceeds of the sales and lay them at the apostles' feet, and they would be distributed to each as any had need.*

The congregation was a unit that worked together with one heart and one soul serving and blessing one another even in times of need.

Perhaps the greatest description in the Bible that relates to the church is the term "brotherhood" (1 Peter 2.17). The church is a family.

One of the biggest decisions your family has to make is which local congregation you will make part of your family.

Blood is Thicker than Water?

I ran an internet search on this phrase to see if I could find out its background. Regrettably, I have yet to uncover any reliable history. However, I have a feeling this phrase was originated during some congregational feud in which people divided along family lines. The fact that all of them had been baptized did not change anything. Blood was thicker than water.

That is extremely sad. Yet, perhaps you have seen this sort of thing happen as well. In contrast, look at Jesus' statement in Matthew 12.46–50. Someone said to Jesus, "Behold, Your mother and Your brothers are standing outside seeking to speak to You." Jesus, however, responded, "Who is My mother and who are My brothers?" Then stretching out His hands to His disciples, He continued, "Behold My mother and My brothers! For whoever does the will of my Father who is in heaven, he is My brother and sister and mother."

Jesus viewed His family as those who submitted to His heavenly Father, not those who were related to His earthly father. Jesus expected us to see the same relationship. In Mark 10.29–30, when Peter had commented about what the apostles had given up to follow Him, Jesus said:

> *There is no one who has left house or brothers or sisters or mother or father or children or farms, for My sake and for the gospel's sake, but that he will receive a hundred times as much now in the present age, houses and brothers and sisters and mothers and children and farms…*

Jesus recognized that becoming a part of His family might cause trouble in our earthly families. In fact, in Matthew 10.35–36, Jesus pointed out that even though we might think everyone in the world would be happy for us to become more Christlike, being a Christian will often turn our earthly families against us. "A man's enemies will be the members of his household." However, we gain a greater family, a family that, when working properly, will stand closer to us than our blood family. When we Christians are behaving like Christ, the waters of baptism are thicker than the blood of family.

Treated Like Family

Hopefully, your blood family has been happy with your decision to be a Christian and even joined you in it. If so, you are doubly blessed. But whether or not this is the case, the brethren in the local congregation are now a part of your extended family. Your family ought to treat them that way.

In 1 Timothy 5.1–2, Paul talked about the way we treat others in the church saying, "Do not sharply rebuke an older man, but rather appeal to him as a father, to the younger men as brothers, the older women as mothers, and the younger women as sisters, in all purity."

Sadly, with as much family mistreatment as occurs today, we may lose the meaning of this verse. Paul was not saying that everyone ought to treat the brethren the way they treat their family. For some, that would be dreadful. Rather, he was saying we ought to treat our brethren in the same positive way we are supposed to treat our family.

Remember Paul's statement in Ephesians 6.1–2, "Children… honor your father and mother." We should treat those who are older with honor, respect and deference. Even if we have to rebuke them, it is to be a love-based appeal filled with respect, rather than a sharp rebuke. Further, this respect for the older brothers and sisters must be engrained in our children. Remember the passage we read in an earlier chapter from Leviticus 19.32, "You shall rise up before the grayheaded and honor the aged…"

Those who are younger should be treated with love and kindness as we would treat our brothers and sisters. As Hebrews 13.2 says, we must "let love of the brethren continue." 1 Peter 3.8 says all Christians are to be "harmonious, sympathetic, brotherly, kindhearted, and humble in spirit." Ephesians 4.31–32 says, "Let all bitterness and wrath and anger and clamor and slander be put away from you, along with all malice. Be kind to one another, tender-hearted, forgiving each other, just as God in Christ also has forgiven you."

When I think about brothers and sisters, especially dealing with younger brothers and sisters, I think about the tendency toward protection. While older brothers and sisters are too often known for personally picking on their younger siblings, they are typically extremely protective of them. We ought to deal with our younger brethren as those younger brothers and sisters that need our help, strength and protection.

Speaking of those younger brethren, I think of Paul's relationship with Titus and Timothy. Paul had taken an integral part in the training of these younger men. As he spoke to them, he treated them as sons. "To Timothy, my true child in the faith..." (1 Timothy 1.2). "To Timothy, my beloved son..." (2 Timothy 1.2). "To Titus, my true child in a common faith..." (Titus 1.4). When John wrote his third letter, he said, "I have no greater joy than this, to hear of my children walking in the truth" (3 John 4).

When we see the family relationship within the local congregation, we recognize everyone in the family is at a different age. Some of them are older and deserve respect. Some of them are younger and need lots of help. As we strengthen those who are young in the faith, we should treat them as we do our children who are young in the flesh.

Consider your children when they were learning how to walk. When little Billy first pulled himself up on the couch and you said, "Come to daddy (mommy)." He let go of the couch and immediately fell over. What did you do? Yell and holler? Ridicule and berate? Demonstrate all manner of disappointment? Grab the rod? Of course not. You encouraged. You praised Billy on what he did right and encouraged him to try again. He failed again and you encouraged some more. We need to remember that regarding children in the faith.

Dysfunctional Families

This chapter has seemed more about the church than the family. However, we must not miss how important this aspect of our family life is. Our family is not to sequester itself from the church family. Rather, it is to be a working unit within the larger whole. Our next chapter will deal with some practical aspects of the relationship between the family and the local congregation. However, for this chapter let's suffice it to say that our family is to be a working, functional and involved part of a local church.

Dysfunctional families receive a lot of press and attention in today's world. Just as bad are the number of dysfunctional church families that exist. What makes a church family dysfunctional? Families like ours when we don't take an active part in the congregation.

1 Corinthians 12, I think, speaks about the universal church. However, its principle and application is most seen in the local church. The church is a body made up of different parts that all function differently—eyes, ears, hands, feet, etc. When any part of the body does not work the way it can and should, the body doesn't function properly. Thus, it becomes a dysfunctional church. Please, do not try to claim your family can't do much. Even if that is true (and it probably is not) Paul wrote, "It is much truer that the members of the body which seem to be weaker are necessary" (vs. 22).

The verse that most stands out to me in this chapter is vs. 18: "But now God has placed the members, each one of them, in the body, just as He desired." That means you and your family are where you are because God knows you can provide something to His body there. The question is—are you doing what God knows you can?

Your Family Needs God's Family

The man had cleaned up his house and was waiting for the elder to arrive. This brother had not attended an assembly in a while and the elder had called him and asked to pay him a visit. The man had agreed because he wanted to tell the elder why he believed he really didn't need the local church. He could be spiritual all on his own. He could pray when he wanted and read his Bible when he wanted. He didn't have to "go to church" to be spiritual.

When the door bell rang, he opened the door and the two men exchanged pleasantries. He ushered the elder into his den to one of the chairs next to his crackling fire. The elder commented on the nice fire, rubbed his hands together in front of it and sat down. He moved to speak several times, but looked as if he were struggling with the right words to say. The man was not going to help him out. He had planned it out in his mind. He would wait until the elder started telling him why he needed to attend the assemblies and then would assail him with his sound individualistic spirituality.

Finally, the elder stared into the fire, arose and picked up the tongs from the hearth. He selected a glowing ember that was two or three inches long. He laid it on the brick hearth and sat back down. He watched, as did the wayward brother, while the ember's bright red glow faded into a dusty gray. Then the elder picked the dead wood back up and placed into the flickering fire. In an instant, the ember glowed bright orange-red again. He looked at the wayward brother with moist eyes. The man, humbled, bowed his head and said, "I will see you on Sunday."

For all the other points we have made about your family and the local family of God, you need to remember this one. God did not command us to attend the assemblies of the local congregation (Hebrews 10.25) to be a burden to us. He did so to be a help. Where else can we go for relief from the pressure of the tempter and his world? Where else can we go to find like-minded people who will lift us up when we are down, heal us when we are hurting and carry us along when we feel defeated? Too many families decide they don't need the local church. They can maintain their spirituality without it. After all, Christianity is about their personal relationship with Christ, isn't it? However, God has made us to be together, to encourage one another, to push one another. You and your family need the local church to stimulate you to love and good deeds (Hebrews 10.24). No matter where you end up, make sure you are always an active part of a local church family.

Today's Response:

With your family, write out all the reasons you work with the congregation of which you are a part.

Point to Ponder:

How important is the local church to you and your family? How important are you and your family to the local church?

Today's Prayer:

Dear Lord,

Thank You for Your blood-bought body. Thank You for the local congregation of which we are a part. We pray Your richest blessing on our family and upon our congregation.

Strengthen us to maintain our commitment to Your body and to the locally body here. Forgive us when we have not functioned in the body as we ought. Help us glorify You in Your body forever.

We love You Father.

Through Your Son we pray,

Amen

Being Involved

The Five, Two and One-Talent Families

You have, no doubt, heard of the Parable of the Talents in Matthew 25.14–30. Consider that story in light of your family. Talents, in this parable, may represent abilities, resources or opportunities—anything useful to serve the Master. How many talents does your family possess?

Too many families tend to have a low estimation of the service they can render the Lord and His church. They believe real service can only be performed by elders, deacons and preachers and their families. That is simply not the case.

However, what if it were true? What if, for sake of argument, your family really is only a one-talent family? What if there really is not a great deal you can accomplish? Maybe you have very limited resources. Maybe your abilities are minimal. Maybe you simply have so few opportunities to serve the Lord you simply can't do much. What should be your family's response to this situation? Should you bury the minimal talent you have and hope the Master will simply be merciful to you? Of course not.

When the master came to the one talent man who buried his talent fearing he could not do anything, the master said,

> *You wicked, lazy slave, you knew that I reap where I did not sow and gather where I scattered no seed. Then you ought to have put my money in the bank, and on my arrival I would have received my money back with interest. Therefore take the talent from him, and give it to the one who has the ten talents. For to everyone who has, more shall be given, and he will have an abundance; but from the one who does not have, even what he does have shall be taken away. Throw out the worthless slave into the outer darkness; in that place there will be weeping and gnashing of teeth (Matthew 25.26–30).*

Even if you are just a one talent family, you need to do what you can. This parable points out that when your family does what God has given the talents for, He will give you more. Therefore, as you consider your relationship with the local church, realize it is not a place to go, it is a community requiring involvement.

The Country Club we mentioned in the last chapter can probably handle it if you only come when you feel like it. It can probably handle it if you do not contribute much but just enjoy the services. Your church family, however, cannot handle that. The church needs you to use your talents to glorify God and serve his people.

Matthew 10.42 says, "Whoever in the name of a disciple gives to one of these little ones even a cup of cold water to drink, truly I say to you, he shall not lose his reward." That may not seem like much to us, but the Lord said we will be rewarded when do what we can, even if what we can do seems small. The rest of this chapter is about the practical ways your family can be involved in working with the local congregation.

The Church's Work

Every congregation is different to some degree. The work available may vary, but differences are usually variations on a theme. In 1 Timothy 3.15, Paul said, "I write so that you will know how one ought to conduct himself in the household of God, which is the church of the living God, the pillar and support of the truth." The church's job is to uphold the truth—uphold it in the sense of following it above all else and also in the sense of holding it for the world to see.

Clearly the main work involved is teaching. There are numerous forms of teaching churches use in which you can help. Probably the first that comes to mind is the Bible classes. Your family can be involved by working with the classes as teachers or assistants. You can help prepare materials or classrooms. You can watch the teachers' or workers' children while they do the preparation. Certainly, you can help by doing your best to always be prepared to participate positively in the classes.

Most churches have some kind of evangelistic work—perhaps a website, a correspondence course, a phone message system, a visitation program or some other means of trying to get the word out systematically. Your family can post announcements about these venues in your community. You can grade correspondence courses, write or record messages, monitor the website, go visiting. Of course, the best thing you can do regarding this is inviting. If the congregation has a website, let your friends and family know about it. Invite people to call your church's phone Bible message system. Most of all, let them know about the assemblies and classes. One of the greatest evangelistic feats recorded in Scripture is when the Samaritan woman at the well went into her city and simply invited the people to come check out the Man she just met who told her about her whole life (cf. John 4.29, 39–42).

One of the great ways to be involved is to be an encouragement to all the others who are involved. Romans 12.10 says, "Be devoted to one another in brotherly love; give preference to one another in honor." 1 Timothy 5.17 says, "The elders who rule well are to be considered worthy of double honor, especially those who work hard at preaching and teaching." Honor the elders. Send them notes of encouragement. Give them phone calls and let them know you appreciate them. Have them into your home. Do the same for deacons, preachers, class teachers, etc.

Let me tell you a story. A man visited one of his favorite restaurants only to find out they had removed fried frog legs from the menu. Since that was the reason he frequented the restaurant, he asked the manager what was the problem. The manager explained that costs were simply too high and he could no longer afford them. The man said, "Well maybe we can work out a deal. I have a pond out beside my house and it has so many frogs in it I could keep you stocked up." They worked out a deal and the man went home to catch a mess of frogs. The next day he returned with a sack containing only two of the green beasts. The restaurant manager was, to say the least, upset. When he questioned the man, he could only reply. "Well, they were making so much noise it sounded like the pond was full, but when I hunted them down it was only these two." In like manner, while most brethren do honor and respect the elders, deacons and preachers and treat them nicely, usually, only the ones who are upset vocalize anything. While there may only be two noisy frogs in the whole pond, it always seems like more. You would be amazed at the benefit the workers in your congregation would have from your words, notes, calls and actions of honor and encouragement, especially if you take the time to get your children involved.

I can tell you from personal experience how awesome these small encouragements can be. I remember a time when I had just been informed by the elders that someone was complaining about my preaching. I was discouraged and disheartened. It was hard to wade through the discouragement to look for any truth in the complaints to reach for improvement. As if by providence, two days later I received a note out of the blue by one of the sisters in the congregation letting me know how much she appreciated me and my family. It was like the clouds parting on a rainy day and the sun shining down on our house. Then there was another time when, sadly enough, some wayward Christians had called the police to get myself and my elders to stop trying to follow up with them. Talk about discouraging. A few days after the elders let the congregation know what had happened, one of my quiet brethren who doesn't say much, dropped by the office for about five minutes to say nothing more than he just wanted to encourage me. I had been struggling with the whole situation. I had been angry, frustrated, grieved and a whole host of other emotions. I had wondered what I did wrong (and I am sure I did something), but the worry was hampering every aspect of my work. It probably took 20 minutes out of this brother's day to stop by my office, but it was exactly what I needed in that moment. You and your family can be this kind of encouragement and you never know when it is needed most, so do it often.

Honor and encourage the others you see working, even the ones who are only able to give a cup of cold water. As Paul said in 1 Corinthians 12.23, "Those members of the body which we deem less honorable, on these we bestow more abundant honor, and our less presentable members become much more presentable." Some may not be able to do as much as your family, but they need to be honored and encouraged as well.

One of the greatest prospects a local church has is the person who has visited one of the classes or assemblies. We only see the tip of the iceberg on these guests. Keep in mind that of the hundreds of things they could have been doing at that moment, they chose to check out your congregation. Your family can be involved by following up with guests. Visit with them at the services. Help them find their classes and fill them in on how things work. Send them a note of appreciation. Give them a call and invite them to come again. Drop by their house with a gift of appreciation. Invite them over (remember the bit about being hospitable to strangers?). Don't wait for an elder or a deacon to assign you this task, just be involved. Of course, don't forget that one of the biggest things you can do for these guests is to be devoted and involved in the worship. As far as the guests are concerned, if the members aren't involved in the worship of the local congregation, why should the guests be?

One of the issues often overlooked in this work of the congregation is upkeep of the facilities. While this is not directly related to teaching, if we are allowed to have facilities (buildings and classrooms) then we have to keep them up. A very strong non-verbal message is sent to non-Christians if they see a run-down building and an overgrown yard. Certainly, people should be so devoted to Christ they don't care what the place of worship looks like. But if they were that devoted, they would already be part of the congregation. Think like an outsider, someone who just wants to get right with God but has no idea what the Bible says and what the differences are between churches. Imagine you were going to buy groceries. You came across two stores just down the street from each other. The sign on one was falling down and not well lit. The grass was overgrown. The building was in bad need of painting. You walked in through glass doors that were dirty and streaked, found walls that were scuffed and dingy, carpet and flooring that was soiled and marked and had trouble seeing because the lighting was bad. Then you went to the other store and found an immaculate building. The sign worked, the outside was freshly painted. The glass was clear, the floors and walls clean, the lighting bright. To which store would you return? That is how non-Christians see congregations. We need to present a positive image. After all, if we do not care about the place in which we worship, what are we telling the community about how worthwhile our worship really is? Sadly, more and more churches have to contract this kind of work out. You and your family can be involved by helping out with the building upkeep—cleaning, mowing, painting, landscaping, repairs, etc.

You knew I would get here—personal studies. Hebrews 5.12 demonstrates natural growth for Christians leads to becoming able to teach. Perhaps you do not feel prepared to do this right now. That is alright. However, you and your family need to work to that goal. We have to understand Christianity is a taught religion. As Romans 10.13–15 demonstrates, no one will be brought to grace in Jesus if we are not teaching them. 1 Peter 3.15 says, "Sanctify Christ as Lord in your hearts, always being ready to make a defense to everyone who asks you to give an account for the hope that is in you, yet with gentleness and reverence." Every family needs to be prepared to give a defense for what they believe. If nothing else, make a list of the verses that provoked you to believe and obey the gospel and be prepared to share it with others.

In addition to this direct work within the local congregation, there is also the involvement you should have with others because they are also part of the congregation. Acts 2.44–47 describes the earliest church:

> *And all those who had believed were together and had all things in common; and they began selling their property and possessions and were sharing them with all as anyone might have need. Day by day continuing with one mind in the temple, and breaking bread from house to house, they were taking their meals together with gladness and sincerity of heart, praising God and having favor with all the people.*

In the above passage, we see the church working together as the church, assembling daily in the temple. Then we see the members involved with one another on a daily basis because they were members of the church together. You and your family need to be involved in this way as well.

Notice the two aspects of this individual involvement. The Christians spent social time together and spiritual time together. Brethren seem to go through cycles of extremes on this issue. On the one hand there are periods when brethren have the idea that every time they get together it must be for a Bible study, singing or prayer. In these times, there is a lot of study and worship, but nobody knows each other and can rarely help each other when they are in spiritual need. Seeing this problem, the pendulum shifts as Christians begin to think, "We are getting enough of the spiritual stuff in our Bible classes and worship assemblies. What we really need is time to get to know one another." They increase social get-togethers and get to know each other better. The problem is for all their knowing each other, they haven't studied much together and are of little help to each other because they do not know their Bible's well enough. We have to find the balance the early Christians practiced.

By the way, if we want to know the truth about getting to know our brethren, we rarely get to know them at parties and socials. We get to know our brethren in times of trial and work. If you really want to get to know your brethren, don't schedule a get together at your home; schedule a work day at one of the widow's homes.

Family Foundations

By way of reminder, my opinion regarding the importance of your family foundation has not changed since chapter five, "Family First." Before you overburden yourself with church work involvement, make sure your family is together and connected. It would be dreadful for you and your family to accomplish all kinds of work with others but then lose each other in the process.Here are a few keys to help you keep that family foundation.

First, schedule your family's personal habits of togetherness, including family worship, study, prayer, teaching, traditions and fun together times.

Second, as you look for ways to be involved in the church's work, look first for work you can do as a family and keep the family involved. Instead of always going to the church building and letting the kids run off to play, find work they can do to help you work together. I know it would be easier for you to do it all yourself, but in the long run you will appreciate it. Obviously, you can't always do this, but do it as often as possible. I remember a day when several families gathered to do some work in preparation for a Vacation Bible School.

The church had printed postcard sized invitations. The families were going to go through the nearby neighborhoods and hang invitation cards on mailboxes. While the parents could have easily shouldered the burden, they didn't. We were there together, kids and all. One brother was punching holes in the cards while the rest of us, including children, looped rubber bands through the holes to make them easier to hang. Granted, sometimes the children would try to sneak off and play. However, for the most part, they had just as much fun laughing and talking while they worked. Then we went off to various neighborhoods and passed out invitations. My children still talk about that day and the work they did for the Lord. At the time they were eight, five and three. It was a great day.

Third, when you have brethren into your home, especially for spiritual activities, keep your entire family involved. Don't send the kids to the playroom to stay out of your hair. Let them sing, pray or study with you. Certainly, teach them how to behave honorably in the presence of adults. While they should be allowed involvement, they have to know respect in the presence of their elders.

Fourth, make sure you are being honest with yourself, your family and your brethren. There are so many opportunities to fill our time with extra-curriculars we are not always aware of what we are doing. Some families get caught up in scouts, sports, band, choir, etc. Then when they are asked to be involved in the church's work, they claim they do not have any more time because they have to keep their family together time. We have to be honest with ourselves here. This is not a situation of choosing to keep the family foundation firm over being involved in church work. This is a choice between secular extra-curricular activities and the Lord's work. Yes, we must prioritize our family foundation in seeking God's kingdom and righteousness. Then we must make sure our families are involved with our extended church family. Once these foundations are laid, we may pursue our heart's desire regarding secular extra-curriculars. We must not let the world, the tempter and personal pleasure steal our time. We have to put the big rocks in first or else we will not have room for them. I cannot draw lines for you regarding when you have laid the foundations. Each family will make its own judgments on these issues and to a great extent we must let them. I am simply convinced when we live by Matthew 6.33 (seek first God's kingdom and righteousness), we will lay those foundations properly.

Remember, the local church is your family. Just as you work to be involved with your earthly family, make sure you are working to be involved with your heavenly family.

Today's Response:

With your family, write out all the ways you are involved in the work of your local church family. Is there anything else you can do to be involved? Schedule it and do it.

Point to Ponder:

Consider the workers in your local church family (even the "cup of cold water" workers). How can you honor and encourage them both great and small?

Today's Prayer:

Father in heaven,

You have blessed our family with abilities, resources and opportunities and we thank You. Help us use these "talents" in a way that pleases and glorifies You. Strengthen us to be prepared for Your Son's return that we might make a return to Him regarding these talents with which He has entrusted us.

Forgive us for when we have not used these "talents" to Your glory and strengthen us to overcome the Tempter.

We love You Father.

Through Your Son we pray,

Amen

Week 2

23

Stewardship

God Loves a Cheerful Giver

Obviously, one aspect of involvement in the local church I overlooked in the last chapter is financial involvement. You have probably heard sermon after sermon and class after class on giving. I am sure you know its principles.

1 Corinthians 16.1–2 demonstrates Christians should contribute to the church's work on the first day of the week, giving as they have been prospered. Under the New Covenant, there is no set amount to give. Further, there is no set percentage to give. However, those who have been blessed with greater income and net worth should be giving more than those with less.

2 Corinthians 9.6–7 demonstrates we should give bountifully, not sparingly. Further, we are to purpose our giving in our hearts. That is, we must not wait until the plate is passed in front of us and just grab whatever comes out of the wallet or purse first. We should plan our giving. Finally, we should give cheerfully, not grudgingly.

That covers the main aspects of giving. Yet, despite how well Christians know all of this, churches are continually in want of funds to accomplish the work they desire for the Lord and sermons on giving are still met with resentment. When trends of giving are measured against average incomes, almost universally Christian giving seems to fall below anything we might possibly consider a standard for giving. Why does that happen? Regrettably, some elders and preachers attack this problem as if most Christians are just not spiritual enough. They hammer away with a constant peppering of guilt inducing sermons to pressure brethren to give more.

In my experience, the issue is rarely one of lack of desire or spirituality on the average Christian's part. Most Christians go home from those kinds of sermons wanting to give more, feeling guilty because they don't see how they can and then led to resentment that a preacher should blast away at them when he doesn't understand the difficult situation they are in.

While sermons on giving need to be preached, we need to actually back up and learn that the real issue is stewardship. Most of us want to be more involved financially in the work of the local church and the Lord. Regrettably, however, few of us were ever taught how to actually manage our financial blessings. Therefore, we always come up short. We feel guilty, but we keep thinking, "When I just get past this point I will be able to give more."

Therefore, this chapter, while helping your family be more financially involved with the local church, is designed to help your family understand principles of stewardship. Whole series of books can and have been written on this subject. We will only hit some highlights.

First Principles of Stewardship

To get the stewardship thing down we have to understand two first principles. If we get these principles under our belts, the rest will fall in line naturally.

The first thing we need to understand is how much of what we have actually is the Lord's. Does He own 10%? 15%? Is it left up to us to determine how much He owns?

The reality is 100% of what we own belongs to God. In Psalm 50.9–12 He said:

> *I shall take no young bull out of your house*
> *Nor male goats out of your folds.*
> *For every beast of the forest is Mine,*
> *The cattle on a thousand hills.*
> *I know every bird of the mountains,*
> *And everything that moves in the field is Mine.*
> *If I were hungry I would not tell you,*
> *For all the world is Mine, and all it contains.*

Additionally, "every good thing given and every perfect gift is from above, coming down from the Father of lights" (James 1.17). Every thing we own and everything we are given is actually God's. As we have called this chapter "Stewardship," we must understand that we are actually stewards of God's things. The house in which we live, the cars we drive, the clothes we wear, the food we eat, the salaries we earn are not our own to do with what we want. They are God's and are to be used to His glory and in His service. That does not mean we are to give 100% of our income and net worth into the church's collection. It does mean that 100% of our income and net worth must be used to glorify and serve God His way.

The second principle is not about our stuff but about us. During the first century, Judea suffered a great famine. Brethren from all over were asked to send assistance to the Jerusalem and Judean Christians. As Paul wrote to the Corinthians to encourage them to help out, he referred to the Macedonian Christians. These had given far beyond anything Paul had expected. However, this giving did not come because they simply understood the principles of giving. They had accomplished something more fundamental, causing their giving and generosity to simply fall into place.

2 Corinthians 8.5 Paul wrote that the Macedonian Christians "first gave themselves to the Lord." The Macedonians were able to give properly from their finances because they had given themselves to God. They were no longer their own, therefore, they no longer strove to maintain their own. They were willing to use themselves and all they had to God's glory and in the service of His people because they knew it belonged to God anyway.

When we get these principles down, all other aspects of stewardship and giving will fall naturally into place.

Why Are We Blessed?

Further, before learning a few keys of proper stewardship, we need to understand why God blesses us financially. Just as God did not bless Israel with the Promised Land because they deserved it, He has not blessed us with jobs, homes, etc. because He owes us.

The Parable of the Talents that we discussed in the last chapter from Matthew 25.14–30 provides one purpose for our blessings. God has blessed us that we might produce a return for Him. As we learned in chapter 7, our purpose as Christ's disciples is to bear fruit glorifying God (John 15.8).

Second, 1 Timothy 5.8 demonstrates God has blessed us that we may provide for our physical needs and those of our family. In fact, if we do not provide for those needs, we are worse than unbelievers.

Third, Ephesians 4.28 said we "must labor, performing with [our] hands what is good, so that [we] will have something to share with the one who has need." 2 Corinthians 9.8 demonstrates this same point saying, "God is able to make all grace abound to you, so that always having all sufficiency in everything, you may have an abundance for every good deed." God has blessed us in order to be a blessing on others, sharing with those who have need.

Fourth, and I am sure you will find this surprising, God has blessed us to be able to enjoy the blessings of His hand. Ecclesiastes 9.7–9 says:

> *Go then, eat your bread in happiness and drink your wine with a cheerful heart; for God has already approved your works. Let your clothes be white all the time, and let not oil be lacking on your head. Enjoy life with the woman whom you love all the days of your fleeting life which He has given to you under the sun; for this is your reward in life and in your toil in which you have labored under the sun.*

God gives us good gifts to enjoy. While we must never horde God's blessings, we must not believe we are not allowed to enjoy His gifts either. While life on earth is not heaven, God has not planned it to be the other alternative either.

Stewardship Highlights

As explained above, this is not the forum for a completely in depth look at stewardship. However, we will cover a few highlights to help our families be better at stewardship and therefore better at our financial involvement in the congregation.

Allow money to be a tool, not a master. In 2 Kings 5, Elisha told Naaman how to be healed of leprosy. When Naaman obeyed and was healed, he wanted to give great gifts to Elisha. Elisha refused. As Naaman left, Elisha's servant Gehazi let his greed get the better of him. Instead of focusing on God's will and glory, Gehazi focused on the material things he could get out of Naaman. However, in the end, Gehazi's greed caused his body to be defiled; he was punished with leprosy. Perhaps Paul had this story in mind when he wrote, "But those who want to get rich fall into temptation and a snare and many foolish and harmful desires which plunge men into ruin and destruction" (1 Timothy 6.9). Money is a tool. We must not allow it to be our master, searching for it and seeking after it at all costs. Its costs are too great.

Trust in God, not in riches. In 1 Timothy 6.17, Paul also wrote about wealth, "Instruct those who are rich in this present world not to be conceited or fix their hope on the uncertainty of riches, but on God, who richly supplies us with all things to enjoy." The week before I have written this chapter, the Gulf Coast was ravaged by hurricane Katrina. New Orleans can barely be described as existing. The rest of the coast through Mississippi and into Alabama is hardly better. Millions are homeless. Reports in my home of Middle Tennessee are about the numbers who have simply fled their homes and are going to start over wherever they end up. Can there be any greater demonstration of Jesus' words in Matthew 6.19? "Do not store up for yourselves treasures on earth, where moth and rust destroy, and where thieves break in and steal. But store up for yourselves treasures in heaven, where neither moth nor rust destroys, and where thieves do not break in or steal." We have to learn to trust God and not material things. The fact is, material things provide only a little in this life and absolutely nothing in the next.

Give to God first. When we are trusting God and not material things, we find it easier to live by this principle. Sometimes we have to give by faith and not by sight. As Proverbs 3.9 says, "Honor the Lord from your wealth and from the first of all your produce." 1 Corinthians 16.2 shows that we should give based on what God has given us, not based on what we have left over. When you are concerned about this, remember Matthew 6.33, "Seek first God's kingdom and righteousness, and all these things will be added to you." When we honor God from the first and best of our material blessings, trusting Him, He will provide for us.

Be generous. Often those who have less look at the rich as if they must be evil. That is simply not the case. 1 Timothy 6.17 demonstrated that Christians might be wealthy. The key to a person's spirituality and their prosperity is not how much they have, but how generous they are with what they are given. 1 Timothy 6.18–19 goes on to say to the rich, "Instruct them to do good, to be rich in good works, to be generous and ready to share, storing up for themselves the treasure of a good foundation for the future, so that they may take hold of that which is life indeed." I am not sure where I first heard the following statement, but it is a good one and applies to us all. "It is not what I would do if a million were my lot, it is what I am doing with the dollar and quarter I've got." Too often those who have less end up being more miserly than the wealthy. We must learn to be generous no matter what our level of blessing.

Budget and plan ahead. No matter how wealthy or blessed we may be, we do not have endless funds. That means we cannot just give and spend indiscriminately. We must not think we can be reckless, even in generosity, and then expect God to pull us out of the fire. Even in finances we must live by the principle of the farm, we reap what we sow (cf. Galatians 6.7). The Proverbs 31 woman is a great example of this principle. She certainly fills the responsibility to be the manager of her home (1 Timothy 5.14). She was obviously a planner. She looked for wool and flax, brought her food from afar, gave food to her household and portions to her maidens. She was an investor and a business woman. She considered fields and bought them, then planted vineyards from her gain. She sold to the tradesmen in the market places. She looked well to the ways of her household. As you plan, plan how you are going to provide for your family. Plan how you are going to allot what you receive—contribution to the church, food, shelter, clothing, bills, savings, investing, benevolence. Then live by your plan.

In addition to planning, the Proverbs 31 woman planned ahead for emergencies. She did not fear the snow, because despite how infrequently it snowed in Jerusalem, she was prepared. She planned ahead. Obviously, we cannot plan for every possible contention and we should not expect money to deliver us from every emergency. We must trust God. However, we need to keep in mind if God has provided for us and we squander it, He is not obligated to miraculously bring us out of emergencies of our own making. We must plan and plan ahead.

Steer clear of consumer credit. This is a tough lesson and one that I am still learning in the school of hard knocks. However God has tried to teach us this lesson through His word. Proverbs 22.7 says, "The borrower becomes the lender's slave." No, this passage does not say borrowing money is sinful. It simply points out the relationship between borrower and lender. It is not a pleasant place to be. Anyone who has to give up several hundred dollars a month to pay for pleasures already past knows this feeling of enslavement. There may be circumstances in which credit is not a bad thing, however, it is better not to slay the albatross than to live with it hung around your neck for years to come.

Teach your children about money. I know we mentioned that in the chapter about "Wisdom and Instruction." However, I have to mention it again. If you don't teach your children how to be good stewards, then you will still be paying for them once they leave the home. That will certainly put a damper on your ability to be a good steward and be financially involved in the local congregation.

*****

Good stewardship is the key to good giving in the local congregation. When we work on stewardship, we can give cheerfully and without guilt knowing we are seeking first God's kingdom and righteousness and using our material blessings to glorify Him. We can have this comfort not only in our giving but in every aspect of our finances.

Today's Response:

Do you have a family spending plan? If so, review it with your children and help them understand how it works. If not, start working on one today. You will need to review this every month to consider special needs and occurrences.

Point to Ponder:

Have you honored God from the first and best of your material blessings? If so, how? If not, what steps must you take to improve?

Today's Prayer:

Benevolent Father,

You have given us good gifts and we thank You. We have abilities, jobs, homes, food, clothing and so much more. You have blessed us far more than we deserve.

Strengthen us to be good stewards of Your blessings. Forgive us for our lack of proper stewardship. Help us keep our faith and trust in You, the Giver, and not in Your gifts. Help us be generous and lay up an eternal treasure and foundation in heaven.

We love You Father.

In Jesus' name we pray,

Amen

Week 5

24

As for Me and My House We Will Serve the Lord

Joshua's Example

As we near the conclusion of our study, we need to summarize all we have learned throughout this book. Perhaps there is no better way than to examine the covenant that occurred in Joshua 24.14–28. I have included the entirety of that text below for easy reference later in the chapter.

> [14] *"Now, therefore, fear the* LORD *and serve Him in sincerity and truth;*
> *and put away the gods which your fathers served beyond the River and*
> *in Egypt, and serve the* LORD. [15] *If it is disagreeable in your sight to serve*
> *the* LORD, *choose for yourselves today whom you will serve: whether the*
> *gods which your fathers served which were beyond the River, or the gods*
> *of the Amorites in whose land you are living; but as for me and my house,*
> *we will serve the* LORD." [16] *The people answered and said, "Far be it from*
> *us that we should forsake the* LORD *to serve other gods;* [17] *for the* LORD
> *our God is He who brought us and our fathers up out of the land of Egypt,*
> *from the house of bondage, and who did these great signs in our sight*
> *and preserved us through all the way in which we went and among all*
> *the peoples through whose midst we passed.* [18] *The* LORD *drove out from*
> *before us all the peoples, even the Amorites who lived in the land. We*
> *also will serve the* LORD, *for He is our God."* [19] *Then Joshua said to the*
> *people, "You will not be able to serve the* LORD, *for He is a holy God. He*
> *is a jealous God; He will not forgive your transgression or your sins.* [20] *If*
> *you forsake the* LORD *and serve foreign gods, then He will turn and do*
> *you harm and consume you after He has done good to you."* [21] *The people*
> *said to Joshua, "No, but we will serve the* LORD." [22] *Joshua said to the*
> *people, "You are witnesses against yourselves that you have chosen for*
> *yourselves the* LORD, *to serve Him." And they said, "We are witnesses."* [23]

> *"Now therefore, put away the foreign gods which are in your midst, and incline your hearts to the LORD, the God of Israel."* [24] *The people said to Joshua, "We will serve the LORD our God and we will obey His voice."* [25] *So Joshua made a covenant with the people that day, and made for them a statute and an ordinance in Shechem.* [26] *And Joshua wrote these words in the book of the law of God; and he took a large stone and set it up there under the oak that was by the sanctuary of the LORD.* [27] *Joshua said to all the people, "Behold, this stone shall be for a witness against us, for it has heard all the words of the LORD which He spoke to us; thus it shall be for a witness against you, so that you do not deny your God."* [28] *Then Joshua dismissed the people, each to his inheritance.*

Joshua's statement in vs. 15, "As for me and my house, we will serve the Lord," has become a standard motto for God-built families. As we sum up all we have learned about allowing God to build and bless our homes, let's examine what the above passage says about our entire household serving the Lord.

Fear the Lord

In Joshua 24.14, Joshua began this section of his address saying, "Fear the Lord." Fearing the Lord is not spiritually correct in our modern "Christian society." Modern religion and its practitioners believe Christianity and Christians have evolved spiritually enough not to be motivated by fear. Many will consider me practically ungodly and un-Christlike to suggest our families should actually fear our Lord.

Even those who dare say we should fear the Lord will temper and weaken this statement by suggesting the fear we should have for the Lord only means to revere and highly esteem Him with awe. That, however, is not the picture the Bible presents.

In Matthew 10.28, Jesus said, "Do not fear those who kill the body but are unable to kill the soul; but rather fear Him who is able to destroy both soul and body in hell." He was not talking about awe and reverence. After the miraculous execution of Ananias and Sapphira in Acts 5, when the text says, "And great fear came over the whole church, and over all who heard of these things" (Acts 5.11), Luke was not talking about reverence and awe. In Philippians 2.12, when Paul taught the Philippians to "work out your salvation with fear and trembling," he was not speaking of reverence and high estimation. Finally, in 2 Corinthians 5.10–11 when Paul described his own actions and said, "We must all appear before the judgment seat of Christ…Therefore, knowing the fear of the Lord, we persuade men," he was not talking about awe.

In each of the above passages, he was talking about fear. Yes, God loves us so much He sent His only begotten to die for us (John 3.16). Yes, He loves us so much He sent His Spirit to reveal His Word for us (2 Peter 1.20–21). Yes, He loves us so much He has been patient, not willing that any should perish but all come to repentance (2 Peter 3.9). But our God is a jealous God and a consuming fire (Exodus 20.5; 34.14; Deuteronomy 4.24 *et al).* His law may have changed from the Old to the New Covenant, but He has not. If we do not serve the Lord we should be terribly afraid.

Most of us do not view fearing God the way the Bible did. We view it from an emotional standpoint. The Bible actually views it from a behavioral standpoint. Fearing God means to walk in God's ways according to Deuteronomy 10.12. It means to follow God and keep His commandments according to Deuteronomy 13.4. It means to serve God and cling to Him based on Deuteronomy 10.20. Fearing God means to do all this because to do otherwise would incur God's wrath. Hebrews 10.26 says, "If we go on sinning willfully after receiving the knowledge of the truth, there no longer remains a sacrifice for sins, but a terrifying expectation of judgment and the fury of a fire which will consume the adversaries." Yes, we and our families should fear that. And because we fear that, serve the Lord.

Serve the Lord in Sincerity and Truth

As Joshua continued his address in vs. 14, he not only said the people should fear the Lord, but also "serve Him in sincerity and truth." Later in the covenant, the people said in vs. 24, "We will serve the Lord our God and we will obey His voice."

It is not enough to claim to serve the Lord, we must do so accurately and without hypocrisy. We have to understand this balance. If we focus too much on simply being sincere, we will be satisfied with emotional spiritualism, but will not serve God His way. That does not glorify Him, as He testified when He struck down Nadab and Abihu for using fire He had not commanded in Leviticus 10.1–3. We do not want to be like the people of Matthew 7.21–23 who were so sincere in their faith they argued with the Lord about it, but were condemned because they had not done the will of God.

On the other hand, if we focus too much on holding the truth, we will be satisfied with a knowledge that we are doctrinally correct, but our lives may not conform to that correct doctrine. This was the problem of the Pharisees. They were so intent on being minutely correct that they neglected the weighty matters of the law; justice, mercy and faith (Matthew 23.23). Jesus rebuked the Pharisees in Matthew 15.8 by referring to Isaiah 29.13. In that passage, God had said the people "honor me with lip service, but they remove their heart far from Me, their reverence for Me consists of tradition learned by rote."

We have to have the balance. We must have our families serve the Lord in truth, learning to accurately serve Him His way and no other, fulfilling our roles as God has outlined. We must also have our families serve the Lord in sincerity, from the heart. Too many are satisfied with simply letting their families know the "religious traditions" regarding the family or the church. That is not enough, we have to know why and serve God from the heart of our faith that what we are doing is right, else it is sin for us (Romans 2.13; 3.20, 28; 14.23).

Put Away Foreign Gods

This may sound odd for today, however, Joshua's address continued in vs. 14 to say, "put away the gods which your fathers served beyond the River and in Egypt, and serve the Lord." Israel was constantly plagued by idolatry. They were forever turning to serve other gods despite what Jehovah had clearly done for them. I believe the reason idolatry appealed so much to the Israelites is when we make up the god, we get to make up the rules. In the end, they were not serving foreign gods so much as they were serving themselves.

While our families today are not very likely to be pulled away from Jehovah by following Ba'al or Zeus (though there is a resurgence of forms of paganism in our culture today), we must still take care to put away our foreign gods. The first of the 10 Commandments was, "You shall have no other gods before Me" (Exodus 20.3). Anything we put ahead of God is an idol. Remember in chapter 3 we learned that we must seek first God's kingdom and righteousness in our family. Anything we seek above God's kingdom and righteousness is an idol for us and we must put it away.

Colossians 3.5 says we should consider our members dead to "greed, which amounts to idolatry." In Philippians 3.19, Paul talked about those "whose god is their appetite." If our families are pursuing anything above God, we need to put that away, whether it be material goods, personal pleasure and entertainment, fame and influence or anything else. We must put those gods away in our family and demonstrate allegiance to God alone above all else.

Incline Your Hearts to the Lord

As Joshua was wrapping up his address and bringing the Israelites to the point of restating their covenant he said, "…put away the foreign gods which are in your midst, and incline your hearts to the Lord, the God of Israel" (Joshua 24.23).

It is not enough to just put away the foreign gods. We must actively pursue connection with the one true and living God. Interestingly, Joshua did not say "incline your hands" or "incline your heads" to God. He said, "Incline your hearts." The Proverbialist advised, "Watch over your heart with all diligence, for from it flow the springs of life" (Proverbs 4.23).

The heart is the beginning of true service. The Pharisees were very good at getting their hands going in the right direction, but their hearts were far from God. Therefore, despite their attempts to stay minutely devoted to God's law, they neglected the weightier matters (Matthew 23.23). Jesus further rebuked them because they worked to look good on the outside but they needed to cleanse the inner man. Jesus said they were as dishes that were cleaned on the outside, but on the inside they were covered with the muck and grime of previous meals. They were as whitewashed tombs that looked like beautiful monuments, but on the inside were full of the stench and decay of death (Matthew 23.25–27). The heart is where service begins. If we and our families incline our hearts to the Lord, our actions will follow.

We incline our hearts to God through worship, devotion, prayer and study. We incline our hearts to God through obedience. We incline our hearts to God by acknowledging Him in all our ways and trusting Him to see us down all our paths. We incline our hearts to God by sanctifying Him in our hearts, setting Him up on the pedestal in our minds to glory and honor Him above all else.

Is your family's heart inclined to the Lord?

We have heard the sermons and been through the classes that brought up Joshua's address and profound statement. The question is are we willing to make the same statement about our family? "As for me and my house, we will serve the Lord."

That is what this whole book has been about—serving God in and through our families.

Today's Response:

Is there anything in your family's life that seems to take precedence over serving God? Allow honest family discussion (you might be amazed at how perceptive children are, knowing what is most important in your family). If there is, list it below. Then cross it out. As a family, discuss how to put God before whatever is on your list.

Point to Ponder:

Joshua based his address on all that God had done for Israel (Joshua 23–24). What has God done for you and your family that warrants serving Him above all else?

Today's Prayer:

Heavenly Father,

You have done great things for us. You have created this world and given us life. You have sent Your Son as a sacrifice to remove our sins. You have given Your word to teach us Your ways. Father, we thank You and love You.

Please forgive us for when we have allowed other things to come before You. Strengthen our family to serve You above all else. Help us glorify You by living Your way in our family.

We love You Father.

In Jesus' name we pray,

Amen

Week 5

25

Blessed and Blessing

Count Your Many Blessings

As we wrap up our study of the family, we would do well to summarize all we have learned by remembering the well known hymn, "Count Your Blessings." It is too easy to be sidetracked by all of the negative things that happen in our world. It is too easy to listen to the news or read the papers and lose sight of the blessings we face.

As I conclude this book, refugees from New Orleans are making their way to different parts of the country following the deluge of their homes. I imagine for those families it is extremely difficult to recognize blessings. Yet, we all need to take the time to count our blessings.

Our families need to count their blessings. Obviously, blessings differ from family to family. Some of the blessings I will mention in this chapter may not be yours. Please, do not be so distracted about not having received all the blessings mentioned as examples here that you miss the blessings you have received. Some have received more and others less, yet all of us have received more than we deserve. Christian families, if we will be able to continue on in this accursed world, must learn to count blessings.

As we consider family blessings, I think of Proverbs 18.22, "He who finds a wife finds a good thing and obtains favor from the Lord." If you are married, you need to count your blessing. Husbands, the truly amazing thing for us is the unbelievable fortune we had in finding a woman who actually tolerates our presence, considering how insensitive and self-centered we can be. Wives, remember the book of Proverbs was written to a son. However, please recognize that as any man who has you for a wife is lucky, you are also blessed to have found a husband.

Psalm 127.3–5 says, "Behold, children are a gift of the Lord, the fruit of the womb is a reward. Like arrows in the hands of a warrior, so are the children of one's youth. How blessed is the man whose quiver is full of them." As I said earlier, I recognize this psalm was written in an agrarian society. More children meant more farm hands and more shepherds. Yet, again, I do not believe this psalm ceased to be true with the Industrial Revolution.

If you have been given children, they are a blessing. They provide joy and happiness in your younger days and, if you train them properly, security and care in your old age.

James 1.17 says every good gift comes from God. Think of the good gifts you have received. Have you eaten today? Are you wearing clothes today? Did you sleep under a roof last night? Did you have air conditioning or heat? Did you get to ride in your car to work or school this morning? Did you have a sink in which to wash dishes? Or better yet a dishwasher? What about a washer and dryer? Do you cook on a stove or do you have a microwave? Do you have a lawnmower to cut your grass? Or better yet, do you have enough money to pay someone else to do it? What amazing blessings all of these things are.

Of course, some will suggest none of the above are really blessings. We worked for all of them. We made money and paid for them. I think of Acts 17.28. "In Him we live and move and exist..." Were you able to roll out of bed this morning and walk to the bathroom to brush your teeth? Were you able to drive to work? Were you able to speak, lift, move, fix, write or do whatever it is you do to work and make money? Where do you think those abilities come from? Who do you think granted you the time to do the work that has made your income and bought your luxuries? Do you remember James 4.13–15?

> *Come now, you who say, "Today or tomorrow we will go to such and such a city, and spend a year there and engage in business and make a profit." Yet you do not know what your life will be like tomorrow. You are just a vapor that appears for a little while and then vanishes away. Instead, you ought to say, "If the Lord wills, we will live and do this or that."*

The mere fact that you are reading this book is an indication of God's blessings in your life. You are still breathing. You are able to see. You are able to read. Or perhaps someone is reading this to you because you are blind. Consider what a blessing your hearing is.

We have only scratched the surface of blessings and these are just the physical ones. What about the spiritual blessings?

According to Ephesians 1.1–14, if you are in Christ you are blessed because you have been chosen by God to be holy and blameless. You have been adopted as children of God. You have been redeemed, purchased and forgiven of your sins. You are an heir of God's inheritance. Having obeyed the gospel, you have been given salvation.

According to Ephesians 2.1–10, though you were dead in your transgressions, God has breathed life into you. He made you alive together with Christ and has raised you up and seated you with Christ in heavenly places.

According to Ephesians 2.18, we have access to the Father. Hebrews 10.19–22 demonstrates the same thing pointing out that in Christ we are able to draw near the throne of God. We are able to lay our petitions and anxieties before Him, because He cares for us (cf. 1 Peter 5.7).

One of the greatest spiritual blessings of all is explained in 1 Corinthians 10.13. God is holding your family in His hand such that Satan will never be able to tempt you beyond what you are able to handle. God will always bless you and your family with a way of escape from every sin. Further, God is always with us and has promised to never abandon His faithful servant (Hebrews 13.5–6). He has promised that nothing can separate us from Him as long as we remain in Christ (Romans 8.33–39). "…neither death, nor life, nor angels, nor principalities, nor things present, nor things to come, nor powers, nor height, nor depth, nor any other created thing, will be able to separate us from the love of God, which is in Christ Jesus our Lord." Through our faith, He is reserving a home in heaven for us (1 Peter 1.4–5).

The reality is our families are more blessed than we deserve or can truly fathom.

Bestow Your Many Blessings

When I was young, my mom cross-stitched a picture that we have framed and usually keep hanging above our bed. (Marita recently rearranged our room and I haven't put up a new nail. The picture is hanging in the hallway right now. I know, I know, I need to go back and brush up on chapter 11 about the Husband's role). The picture is of a house between two flowering trees. Birds hover over the house clutching a spring garland. Above the picture are the cross-stitched words, "The love in your heart wasn't put there to stay. Love isn't love till it's given away."

The same thing should be said about our blessings. Our families are blessed. Your family is blessed. However, God has not given us those blessings to horde. Yes, we are allowed to enjoy them, but God has blessed us that we may be a blessing. We are to be funnels opened wide to heaven to receive God's blessing, but equally able to pass those blessings along to others. Further, as 2 Corinthians 1.3; Ephesians 1.3 and 1 Peter 1.3 demonstrate, we are to bless God as well.

How can we be a blessing to God and others?

Psalm 34.1–3 says:

> *I will bless the Lord at all times;*
> *His praise shall continually be in my mouth.*
> *My soul will make its boast in the Lord;*
> *The humble will hear it and rejoice.*
> *O magnify the Lord with me.*
> *And let us exalt His name together.*

As we learned in our chapters on habits of the God-built home, our families must be filled with praise. Prayer and singing should fill our homes as we bless God, praising and magnifying Him. Our boast should be in the Lord (1 Corinthian 1.31; 2 Corinthians 10.17), not our strength, wisdom or accomplishment. We should recognize and declare that anything we have accomplished has been by the grace and strength of the Lord. As we have learned from Ephesians 3.20–21, God can do amazing things through the power working in us—His power working in us. Consider Paul's example in 1 Corinthians 3.5. He attributed the work he had done in Corinth to opportunities provided by the grace of God.

Our homes should be places of honor and reverence for God. Neither He nor His church nor His word should be taken lightly, mocked or neglected. We should bless the Lord with our families at home and with our families in the congregation.

Finally, we bless the Lord by obeying Him. The goals, roles, responsibilities and habits we have learned throughout this study are the means by which we bless God. When we bless God in our families we will hear those words spoken regarding the Old Testament faithful in Hebrews 11.16: "Therefore God is not ashamed to be called their God; for He has prepared a city for them." Are our families a blessing to God? Is your family a blessing to God?

Of course, as we become a blessing to others, we further bless God. Keep in mind all we have learned throughout this book about being a blessing to others. Your family can be a team for the Lord to accomplish His work in and among our brethren.

As Galatians 6.9–10 said, "While we have opportunity, let us do good to all people, and especially to those who are of the household of the faith." Our families need to be little teams of servants going about doing good for all we can, whether it be friends, extended family, neighbors, but especially brethren.

As Tabitha in Acts 9.36–43 did what she could by making garments for the widows, our families should serve in whatever way we can, blessing the lives of others. How many widows could use our help in keeping their homes clean? How many elderly could use visits from us and our children to brighten their days? How many others could use help cutting their grass, washing their car or babysitting their kids? What blessings our families could be as servants.

As we consider the blessing of God's presence and comfort, we can be a blessing to others as we extend the comfort of the Lord to them in their times of need. Paul said in 2 Corinthians 1.3–4, "Blessed be the…God of all comfort, who comforts us in all our affliction so that we will be able to comfort those who are in any affliction with the comfort with which we ourselves are comforted by God." As we looked to our blessed hope of eternity with Christ, we can comfort others pointing them to that day when we will be with Christ forevermore as Paul said in 1 Thessalonians 4.17–18. Our words must be a gift of grace and blessing to those who hear us and we must train up our families to speak with grace (Ephesians 4.29).

As the brethren in first century Macedonia did, we must first give ourselves and our families to the Lord and then to our brethren by the will of the Lord (2 Corinthians 8.5). As Paul goes on to say in 2 Corinthians 8.13–14, this is not so others might be at ease while we afflict ourselves. Rather, by means of equality, when we have an abundance, we can help those in need. The day may come when roles are reversed. When we are in need, others will be able to provide for us out of their abundance.

Finally, our homes should be a place of blessing for others. As Lydia and the Philippian Jailer did in Acts 16, our homes should be open to our brethren. Our homes should be a place of teaching and prayer to bless our brethren as we see exemplified in Acts 12.12 as Mary the mother of John Mark opened her home to be a place of prayer. We also see it exemplified by the Ephesians in Acts 20.20 as untold numbers opened their homes to be places of teaching. Like the first Christians in Jerusalem, we should open our homes as places for Christians to pray, sing, study and worship God. Also, our homes should be open to simply spend time together with one another, taking our meals with gladness and enjoying one another's company (Acts 2.46–47). We Christian families must recognize that the headquarters of our work for the Lord is not the church building, it is our homes. Let's make our homes a blessing for our family and for our brethren.

*****

May God continue to bless our families as we study and grow closer to Him. More importantly, may our families bless God and bless God's children. That has been the true intention of this study.

Today's Response:

Make a list of the ways God has blessed your family:

Make a list of the ways your family can bless God and His children:

Point to Ponder:

How many of our blessings do we deserve? Why is it so hard for us to count our blessings?

Today's Prayer:

Merciful Father,

We will bless Your name forever, O Lord, creator of heaven and earth. We will bless You in our home and we will bless You in the assembly. We will bless You in the presence of Your children, the nations and Your enemies. You are worthy of praise, honor and glory.

Father, we pray that You strengthen us not only to be a blessing to You but to Your children. Bless our families that we will be what You have asked us to be.

We love You Father.

In Jesus' name we pray,

Amen

Week Five Group Discussion

- What are the most important lessons you have learned this week?

- What questions do you have about what you learned this week?

- What practical improvement have you and your family made in your family lives based on what you learned this week?

- What practical advice would you give others to accomplish what you learned about this week?

- With what issues do you and your family need help or prayers based on what you learned this week?

- How can our families be more involved in the local church, being a blessing to God and to His children?

- What are the most important lessons you have learned from this entire study over the past month

Conclusion

"How important is your family? What are you willing to do to make your family stable and functional? Are you willing to work long hours to provide materially for your family? Are you willing to rise up early and stay up late to accomplish all the goals and activities in which your family is involved? Are you willing to eat the bread of painful labors to give your children a better life? Are you willing to pursue education, material goods, comfort and recreation for your family? Will you read books? …watch videos? …visit counselors? How important is a stable and functional family to you?

"Here is the important question: Is having a stable and functional family important enough to allow the Lord to build your home?

Unless the Lord builds the house,
They labor in vain who build it;
Unless the Lord guards the city,
The watchman keeps awake in vain.
It is vain for you to rise up early,
To retire late,
To eat the bread of painful labors;
For he gives to His beloved even in his sleep
Psalm 127.1–2

"All of the things we are willing to do to stabilize and functionalize our families are no more than wheel-spinning unless we are willing to allow God to come into our homes, building them and guarding them His way. Are we willing to allow that?"

You may remember the above paragraphs are where we started. I hope this study has been a blessing to you and your family. I hope it has helped you desire and plan to do what is necessary to have a stable and functional family. I hope it has helped you invite God to build your home or increased His involvement.

My prayer is for the families of all my brethren. I pray we will stand out in this world as shining lights, homes set on hills that cannot be hidden. Please pray for me and my family as we continue to grow in all of these principles.

May God richly bless us as we draw closer to Him. More importantly, may we richly bless God.

Edwin L. Crozier

ALSO FROM DEWARD PUBLISHING:

Beneath the Cross: Essays and Relfections on the Lord's Supper
Jady S. Copeland and Nathan Ward (editors)

The Bible has much to say about the Lord's Supper. Almost every component of this memorial is rich with meaning—meaning supplied by Old Testament foreshadowing and New Testament teaching. The Lord's death itself is meaningful and significant in ways we rarely point out. In sixty-nine essays by forty different authors, Beneath the Cross explores the depths of symbolism and meaning to be found in the last hours of the Lord's life and offers a helpful look at the memorial feast that commemorates it. 329 pages. $14.99 (PB); $23.99 (HB).

Invitation to a Spiritual Revolution
Paul Earnhart

Few preachers have studied the Sermon on the Mount as intensively or spoken on its contents so frequently and effectively as the author of this work. His excellent and very readable written analysis appeared first as a series of articles in *Christianity Magazine.* By popular demand it is here offered in one volume so that it can be more easily preserved, circulated, read, reread and made available to those who would not otherwise have access to it. Foreword by Sewell Hall. 173 pages. $10.99 (PB)

Boot Camp: Equipping Men with Integrity for Spiritual Warfare
Jason Hardin

According to Steve Arterburn, best-selling author of *Every Man's Battle,* "This is a great book to help us men live opposite of this world's model of man." *Boot Camp* is the first volume in the IMAGE series of books for men. It serves as a Basic Training manual in the spiritual war for honor, integrity and a God-glorifying life. 237 pages, $13.99 (PB); $24.99 (HB).

Flight Paths: A Devotional Guide to Your Journey
Dene Ward

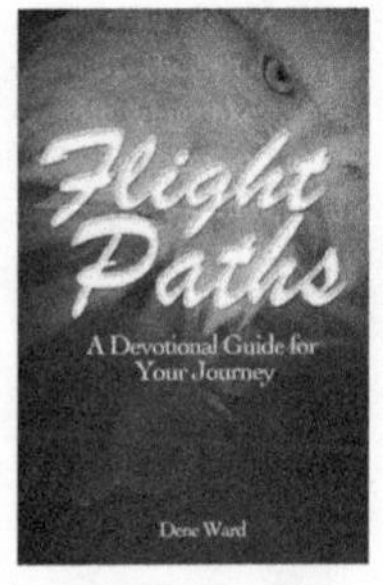

When encroaching blindness took her music teaching career away, Dene Ward turned her attention to writing. What began as e-mail devotions to some friends grew into a list of hundreds of subscribers. Three hundred sixty-six of those devotions have been assembled to form this daily devotional. Follow her through a year of camping, bird-watching, medical procedures, piano lessons, memories, and more as she uses daily life as a springboard to thought-provoking and character-challenging messages of endurance and faith. 475 pages. $18.99 (PB).

The Slave of Christ
Seth Parr

Immerse yourself in a place where sacrifice is reasonable, love and action are sensible, victory is guaranteed, and evangelism explodes. While the sacrifice of Jesus opens the door for us to Heaven, we must work to be conformed into His very image. In The Slave of Christ, uncover what biblical service means and how it can change your life. Energize your spiritual walk and awaken the servant within. 96 pages. $8.99 (PB)

Churches of the New Testament
Ethan R. Longhenry

Have you ever wondered what it would be like to be a Christian in the first century, to meet with the church in Philippi or Ephesus? *Churches of the New Testament* explores the world of first century Christianity by examining what Scripture reveals about the local churches of God's people. It examines background information about the geography and history of each city, as well as whatever is known about the founding of the church there. Centuries may separate us from the churches of the New Testament, but their examples, instruction, commendation, and rebukes can teach us today. 150 pages. $9.99 (PB)

For a full listing of DeWard Publishing Company books, visit our website:

www.deward.com

CPSIA information can be obtained
at www.ICGtesting.com
Printed in the USA
LVHW110744010422
714871LV00001B/38

9 781936 341214